HAL LEONARD

Pocket Guitar Chord Dictionary

by Andrew DuBrock

ISBN 978-1-4234-8501-8

7777 W. BLUEMOUND RD. P.O. BOX 13819 MILWAUKEE, WI 53213

In Australia contact:
Hal Leonard Australia Pty. Ltd.
4 Lentara Court
Cheltenham, Victoria, 3192 Australia
Email: ausadmin@halleonard.com.au

Visit Hal Leonard Online at
www.halleonard.com

Table of Contents

Introduction

The *Pocket Guitar Chord Dictionary* is an extensive reference guide to over 2,700 chords. Fifty-eight different chord qualities are covered for each key, and each chord quality is presented in four different voicings, with the most common one listed first. Open strings are used, but at least one voicing from each quality is a moveable form. This allows for many unique voicings but also provides practical chord forms that can be transposed to any root. For ease of readability, all sharp/flat chord names are labeled with the appropriate flat name. The enharmonic sharp name can be substituted, and is listed at the top of each page. For each voicing, an "R" along the bottom identifies the root note (though some voicings are rootless).

No book would be long enough to include every possible voicing for each chord type. However, many chord types in this book show different moveable forms for each root. If you want to find another voicing for a chord, try looking under a different root name and transposing that shape to the root you're working with.

Keep in mind that different chord types may share the same shape (see the *chord construction* section for an explanation).

A fingerboard chart of the guitar neck is shown below for reference.

	1	2	3	4	5	6	7	8	9	10	11	12
E	F	F#/Gb	G	G#/Ab	A	A#/Bb	B	C	C#/Db	D	D#/Eb	E
B	C	C#/Db	D	D#/Eb	E	F	F#/Gb	G	G#/Ab	A	A#/Bb	B
G	G#/Ab	A	A#/Bb	B	C	C#/Db	D	D#/Eb	E	F	F#/Gb	G
D	D#/Eb	E	F	F#/Gb	G	G#/Ab	A	A#/Bb	B	C	C#/Db	D
A	A#/Bb	B	C	C#/Db	D	D#/Eb	E	F	F#/Gb	G	G#/Ab	A
E	F	F#/Gb	G	G#/Ab	A	A#/Bb	B	C	C#/Db	D	D#/Eb	E

The chords throughout this book are presented in chord grid fashion. In case you're not familiar with this type of notation, below is a detailed explanation of how they're read.

The six vertical lines represent the six strings on the guitar. They are arranged low to high from left to right.

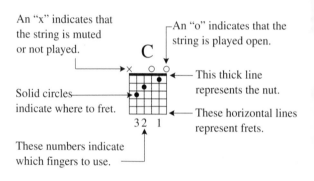

An "x" indicates that the string is muted or not played.

An "o" indicates that the string is played open.

This thick line represents the nut.

Solid circles indicate where to fret.

These horizontal lines represent frets.

These numbers indicate which fingers to use.

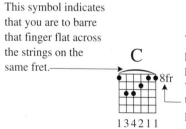

This symbol indicates that you are to barre that finger flat across the strings on the same fret.

When a chord is not played in open position, a fret marker will indicate where on the neck it is to be played.

Chord Qualities

Following is a list of the fifty-eight chord qualities presented in this book, their abbreviations, and their formulas. Many of the extended chords omit one or more notes (see the *chord construction* section for more information on this).

CHORD TYPE	SYMBOL	FORMULA
Major	C	1–3–5
Minor	Cm	1–♭3–5
Diminished	C°	1–♭3–♭5
Augmented	C+	1–3–♯5
Dominant Seventh	C7	1–3–5–♭7
Seventh, Flat Fifth	C7♭5	1–3–♭5–♭7
Seventh, Sharp Fifth	C7♯5	1–3–♯5–♭7
Seventh, Flat Ninth	C7♭9	1–3–5–♭7–♭9
Seventh, Sharp Ninth	C7♯9	1–3–5–♭7–♯9
Seventh, Flat Ninth, Flat Fifth	C7$^{♭9}_{♭5}$	1–3–♭5–♭7–♭9
Seventh, Flat Ninth, Sharp Fifth	C7$^{♭9}_{♯5}$	1–3–♯5–♭7–♭9
Seventh, Sharp Ninth, Sharp Eleventh	C7$^{♯9}_{♯11}$	1–3–5–♭7–♯9–♯11
Seventh, Sharp Ninth, Sharp Fifth	C7$^{♯9}_{♯5}$	1–3–♯5–♭7–♯9
Major Seventh	Cmaj7	1–3–5–7
Major Seventh, Flat Fifth	Cmaj7♭5	1–3–♭5–7
Major Seventh, Sharp Fifth	Cmaj7♯5	1–3–♯5–7
Major Seventh, Sharp Ninth, Sharp Eleventh	Cmaj7$^{♯9}_{♯11}$	1–3–5–7–♯9–♯11
Minor Seventh	Cm7	1–♭3–5–♭7
Minor Seventh, Flat Fifth	Cm7♭5	1–♭3–♭5–♭7
Minor, Major Seventh	Cm(maj7)	1–♭3–5–7
Diminished Seventh	C°7	1–♭3–♭5–♭♭7
Ninth	C9	1–3–5–♭7–9
Ninth, Flat Fifth	C9♭5	1–3–♭5–♭7–9
Ninth, Sharp Fifth	C9♯5	1–3–♯5–♭7–9
Major Ninth	Cmaj9	1–3–5–7–9
Minor Ninth	Cm9	1–♭3–5–♭7–9

CHORD TYPE	SYMBOL	FORMULA
Minor Ninth, Flat Fifth	Cm9♭5	1–♭3–♭5–♭7–9
Minor, Major Ninth	Cm(maj9)	1–♭3–5–7–9
Eleventh	C11	1–3–5–♭7–9–11
Major Eleventh	Cmaj11	1–3–5–7–9–11
Minor Eleventh	Cm11	1–♭3–5–♭7–9–11
Thirteenth	C13	1–3–5–♭7–9–11–13
Thirteenth, Sharp Eleventh	C13#11	1–3–5–♭7–9–#11–13
Thirteenth, Flat Ninth	C13♭9	1–3–5–♭7–♭9–11–13
Thirteenth, Sharp Ninth	C13#9	1–3–5–♭7–#9–11–13
Major Thirteenth	Cmaj13	1–3–5–7–9–11–13
Major Thirteenth, Sharp Flat Fifth	Cmaj13#11	1–3–5–7–9–#11–13
Minor Thirteenth	Cm13	1–♭3–5–♭7–9–11–13
Minor Thirteenth, Flat Fifth	Cm13♭5	1–♭3–♭5–♭7–9–13
Sixth	C6	1–3–5–6
Six-Nine	C⁶/₉	1–3–5–6–9
Minor Sixth	Cm6	1–♭3–5–6
Minor Six-Nine	Cm⁶/₉	1–♭3–5–6–9
Fifth (Power Chord)	C5	1–5
Suspended Second	Csus2	1–2–5
Suspended Fourth	Csus4	1–4–5
Suspended Second and Fourth	Csus²/₄	1–2–4–5
Seventh, Suspended Fourth	C7sus4	1–4–5–♭7
Ninth, Suspended Fourth	C9sus4	1–4–5–♭7–9
Thirteenth, Suspended Fourth	C13sus4	1–4–5–♭7–9–13
Add Fourth	Cadd4	1–3–4–5
Add Ninth	Cadd9	1–3–5–9
Minor, Add Ninth	Cm(add9)	1–♭3–5–9
Flat Fifth	C(♭5)	1–3–♭5
Flat Sixth	C(♭6)	1–3–5–♭6
Seventh, No Third	C7(no 3rd)	1–5–♭7
Ninth, No Third	C9(no 3rd)	1–5–♭7–9
Thirteenth, No Third	C13(no 3rd)	1–5–♭7–9–13

Chord Construction

You don't need to know theory to play music, but it can help you better understand the music you play.

Triads

Triad is a Greek word that means "three," and that's exactly what a triad contains—three notes! Triads are the most common type of chord. They are built by stacking two 3rds on top of each other. When we say "3rds," we're talking about *intervals*—the distance between notes. If you start on one note and move up the scale, the distance between the first note and the next note is a 2nd. The distance between the first note and the third note is a 3rd; between the first and fourth is a 4th, and so on. Thirds can be either major or minor, and stacking these 3rds on top of each other in different combinations creates four types of triads: major, minor, diminished and augmented. Here is what's known as a C Major triad:

The defining note of a chord (its letter name) is called the root. Notice how the second note in the triad is the 3rd. The top note is called the 5th because its interval from the root is a 5th (count up yourself to see). After we take a closer look at intervals, we'll look at the different types of triads you can build with those intervals.

Intervals

The *triad* section briefly mentioned that an interval is the distance between any two notes. Counting up from the first note to the second note will give you the interval between those two notes. That distance is quantified with a number, but intervals also have another component: *quality*. The quality of any interval can be major, minor, diminished, augmented, or perfect. Looking at the twelve notes in a chromatic scale, along with their intervals, can help explain the differences between these qualities:

| tonic (root) | minor 2nd | major 2nd | minor 3rd | major 3rd | perfect 4th | augmented 4th (F♯) *or* diminished 5th (G♭) | perfect 5th | augmented 5th (G♯) *or* minor 6th (A♭) | major 6th | minor 7th | major 7th |

You may notice that every minor interval is one half step smaller than its major-interval counterpart. The only intervals that are not major or minor are the *perfect* intervals: the 4th and 5th. Lowering a perfect interval (like the 5th) results in a diminished interval, while raising a perfect interval (like the 4th) results in an augmented interval. All the other non-perfect intervals can be diminished or augmented as well, though it rarely happens.

Now let's look at all the different types of triads we can build with these intervals. There are four types: major, minor, diminished, and augmented. Major triads have a major 3rd and a perfect 5th; minor triads have a minor 3rd and a perfect 5th; diminished triads have a minor 3rd and a diminished 5th; and augmented triads have a major third and an augmented 5th:

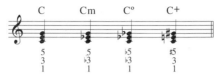

Major triads are labeled with just a letter (C), minor triads are labeled with a lowercase "m" (Cm), diminished traids are labelled with a ○ symbol (C°), augmented chords are labeled with a "+" (C+).

7th Chords

Seventh chords are four-note chords that stack a 7th interval on top of a triad. There are five types of 7th chords: dominant 7th (labeled with a "7" after the chord's letter name), minor seventh (m7), major seventh (maj7), minor-major 7th [m(maj7)], and diminished 7th (°7). Here are the 7th chords with a C root:

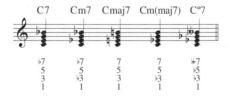

Extended Chords

Beyond 7th chords, you can add further extensions to color the chord even more. Basically, you continue stacking 3rds on top of a 7th chord to build extended chords. Stack one 3rd on top and you have a 9th chord, add a 3rd to the 9th chord and you have an 11th chord, and add a 3rd to that 11th chord to get a 13th chord.

Not all notes of an extended chord are necessary to complete the chord. This is especially true on guitar, where a full 13th chord would be impossible to play. But some of the notes are more important to include than others. For a chord to be an extended chord, you have to include the 3rd, 7th, and the extension. After that, including the 3rd, root and other extensions holds lesser priority. The least important note in an extended chord is the 5th.

It's also important to note that extensions can appear in a different octave than their numerical name implies. For instance, a 13th down one octave is a 6th, but it will still be considered a 13th chord as long as you have a 7th in the chord, as well.

Suspended, Add, and Other Chords

Suspended chords (sus) are formed when a note is substituted for the 3rd. In a sus4 chord, for instance, the 4th is substituted for the 3rd. *Add* chords are ones that add one or more notes to a triad. The difference between a sus4 and an add4 chord, for example, is that the sus4 does not include the 3rd, while the add4 does.

Of course, like the English Language, there are always a few exceptions. A triad with an added 6th is simply called a 6th chord (though it could be written as an add6 chord), and a chord with the 6th and 9th added is simply called a 6/9 chord.

Altered Chords

Any chord can be altered, and that alteration is reflected in the chord's name. For instance, if you alter a 7th chord by lowering the 5th one half step, you have a 7♭5 chord; raise the 5th of that 7th chord by one half step, and you have a 7♯5 chord.

Inversions

Some of the chords in this book are voiced in *inversion*. Any time the lowest note in a chord is *not* the root, the chord is in an inversion. The more notes you have in a chord, the more possible inversions you have. For instance, a triad, which has three different notes, can be voiced in *root position* (root on bottom), *first inversion* (3rd on bottom), or s*econd inversion* (5th on bottom). However, a 7th chord, which has four different notes, can be voiced these three ways as well as *third inversion* (7th on bottom).

Same Shapes, Different Names

Many chords can be called more than one name. For instance, a ♭5th is equivalent to a ♯11, and a chord containing one of these notes could be labeled either way. Keep this in mind if you're unable to find the chord type you're looking for; you may find it by looking up its enharmonic equivalent.

C

Triads

Major

C
× ○ ○
3 2   1
R

C
×
1 3 3 3 1
R

C
8fr
1 3 4 2 1 1
R

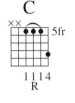

C
× ×
5fr
1 1 1 4
R

Minor (m, -)

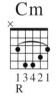

Cm
×
1 3 4 2 1
R

Cm
× ×   ×
5fr
2   1 4
R

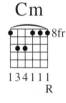

Cm
8fr
1 3 4 1 1 1
R

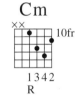

Cm
× ×
10fr
1 3 4 2
R

Diminished (○, dim)

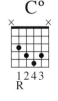

C○
×   ×
1 2 4 3
R

C○
× × ×
7fr
2 1 3
R

C○
× ×
8fr
1 3 4 2
R

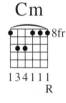

C○
× × ×
11fr
1 3 1
R

C

Augmented (+, aug)

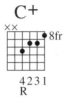
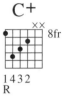

C+   C+   C+   C+

4 3 1 2
R

3 2 1 1
R

4 2 3 1
R

1 4 3 2
R

Seventh Chords

Dominant Seventh (7)

C7   C7   C7   C7

3 2 4 1
R

1 3 1 4 1
R

1 3 1 2 4 1
R

1   2 4 3
R

Dominant Seventh Chords with Alterations

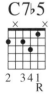
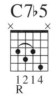

C7♭5   C7♭5   C7♭5   C7♭5

2   3 4 1
R

1 2 1 4
R

1 2 3 4
R

2   3 4 1
R

C

C7#5

1 2 3 4
R

C7#5

1 2 4 3
R

C7#5

1 3 4 2
R

C7#5

2 3 1 4
R

C7b9

2 1 3 1
R

C7b9

T 1 3 2 4
R

C7b9

2 1 3 1

C7b9

2 1 3 1
R

C7#9

2 1 3 4
R

C7#9

1 3 3 3

C7#9

2 1 3 4
R

C7#9

1 2 4 3

C

$C7^{\flat 9}_{\flat 5}$

2 1 3 1 1
R

$C7^{\flat 9}_{\flat 5}$

6fr

3 4 1 2
R

$C7^{\flat 9}_{\flat 5}$

7fr

T 2 3 1 4
R

$C7^{\flat 9}_{\flat 5}$

4fr

1 3 2 4

$C7^{\flat 9}_{\sharp 5}$

2 1 3 1 4
R

$C7^{\flat 9}_{\sharp 5}$

8fr

1 2 3 3 3
R

$C7^{\flat 9}_{\sharp 5}$

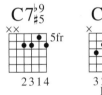
5fr

2 3 1 4

$C7^{\flat 9}_{\sharp 5}$

9fr

3 2 1 4 1
R

$C7^{\sharp 9}_{\sharp 11}$

2 1 3 4 1
R

$C7^{\sharp 9}_{\sharp 11}$

7fr

2 1 3 4 1
R

$C7^{\sharp 9}_{\sharp 11}$

7fr

1 3 4 4 4
R

$C7^{\sharp 9}_{\sharp 11}$

1 2 1 4 5
R

C

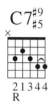

C7$^{\sharp 9}_{\sharp 5}$

×

2 1 3 4 4
R

C7$^{\sharp 9}_{\sharp 5}$

× 7fr

2 1 3 3 3
R

C7$^{\sharp 9}_{\sharp 5}$

× × 8fr

1 2 2 4

C7$^{\sharp 9}_{\sharp 5}$

× ×

1 2 3 4

Major Seventh (maj7, M7, ma7, △7)

Cmaj7

× ○○○

3 2
R

Cmaj7

×

1 3 2 4 1
R

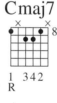

Cmaj7

× × 8fr

1   3 4 2
R

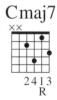

Cmaj7

× ×

2 4 1 3
R

Major Seventh Chords with Alterations

Cmaj7♭5

7fr

2 1 4 3 1 1
R

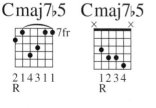

Cmaj7♭5

×

1 2 3 4
R

Cmaj7♭5

× × 4fr

1 2 2 4
R

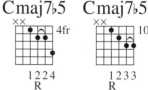

Cmaj7♭5

× × 10fr

1 2 3 3
R

C

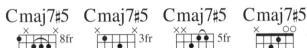

Cmaj7#5

1 333
R

Cmaj7#5

8fr

1423
R

Cmaj7#5

5fr

2114
R

Cmaj7#5

321
R

Cmaj7$^{\sharp 9}_{\sharp 11}$

Cmaj7$^{\sharp 9}_{\sharp 11}$

Cmaj7$^{\sharp 9}_{\sharp 11}$

Cmaj7$^{\sharp 9}_{\sharp 11}$

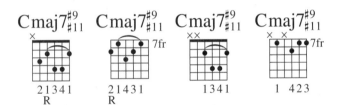

21341
R

7fr

21431
R

1341
R

7fr

1 423

Minor Seventh (m7, min7, -7)

Cm7

13121
R

Cm7

8fr

131111
R

Cm7

4fr

2314
R

Cm7

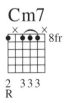

8fr

2 333
R

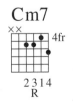

C

Minor Seventh Chords with Alterations

Cm7♭5

1 3 2 4
R

Cm7♭5

7fr

2 3 4 1
R

Cm7♭5

1 3 1 2
R

Cm7♭5

4fr

1 2 1 4
R

Minor-Major Seventh [m(maj7), m/M7]

Cm(maj7)

1 4 2 3 1
R

Cm(maj7)

8fr

1 3 2 1 1 1
R

Cm(maj7)

8fr

1   4 2 3
R

Cm(maj7)

1 4 1 3
R

Diminished Seventh (°7)

C°7

2 3 1 4
R

C°7
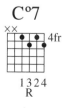

4fr

1 3 2 4
R

C°7

7fr

2   1 3 1
R

C°7

5fr

2   1 4 1
R

C

Ninth Chords
Dominant Ninth (9)

C9

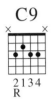

2 1 3 4
R

C9

7fr

1 3 2 4

C9

1 3 3 3

C9

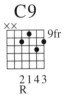

9fr

2 1 4 3
R

Dominant Ninth Chords with Alterations

C9♭5

2 1 3 4 1
R

C9♭

7fr

1 2 1 1 3
R

C9♭5

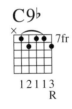

7fr

3 4 1 2
R

C9♭5

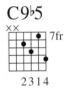

7fr

2 3 1 4

C9♯5

2 1 3 3 4
R

C9♯5

8fr

1 2 3 3 4
R

C9♯5

7fr

1 2 1 4

C9♯5

4 1 2 3

C

Major Ninth (maj9, M9, ma9, △9)

Cmaj9

2 1 4 3
R

Cmaj9

7fr
2 1 4 1 3
R

Cmaj9

12fr
4 1 1 1 1
R

Cmaj9

8fr
1 2 3 4
R

Minor Ninth (m9, min9, -9)

Cm9

2 1 3 4
R

Cm9

8fr
2 3 3 3 4
R

Cm9

8fr
4 1 3 1
R

Cm9

8fr
2 1 4 3
R

Minor Ninth Chords with Alterations

Cm9♭5

6fr
1 3 2 2 4
R

Cm9♭5

8fr
1 2 1 1 4 3

Cm9♭5

1 3 4 2

Cm9♭5

11fr
2 1 1 1

C

Minor-Major Ninth [m(maj9), m/M9]

Cm(maj9)
2 1 4 3
R

Cm(maj9)
8fr
1 3 2 1 1 4
R

Cm(maj9)
3fr
4 3 2 1

Cm(maj9)
8fr
2 1 4 3
R

Eleventh Chords

Dominant Eleventh (11)

C11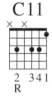
2 3 4 1
R

C11
1 1 1 1 1
R

C11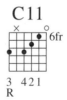
6fr
3 4 2 1
R

C11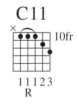
10fr
1 1 1 2 3
R

Major Eleventh (maj11, M11, ma11, △11)

Cmaj11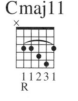
2 1 4 3 1
R

Cmaj11
1 1 2 3 1
R

Cmaj11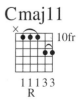
6fr
3 4 2 1
R

Cmaj11
10fr
1 1 1 3 3
R

C

Minor Eleventh (m11, min11, -11)

Cm11
21341
R

Cm11
10fr
11133
R

Cm11
11121
R

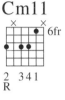
Cm11
6fr
2 341
R

Thirteenth Chords

Dominant Thirteenth (13)

C13
8fr
1 234
R

C13
21334
R

C13
8fr
1231
R

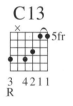
C13
5fr
3 4211
R

Dominant 13th Chords with Alterations

C13#11
12134
R

C13#11
5fr
24131
R

C13#11
5fr
3421
R

C13#11
8fr
121341
R

C

C13♭9

3 4211
R

C13♭9

1214

C13♭9

1243

C13♭9

1333

C13♯9

1234

C13♯9

21334
R

C13♯9

1234

C13♯9

1224

Major Thirteenth (maj13, M13, ma13, △13)

Cmaj13

1 234
R

Cmaj13

3 4211
R

Cmaj13

13244
R

Cmaj13

2341
R

C

Major 13th Chords with Alterations

Cmaj13♯11

1 2 2 2 4
R

Cmaj13♯11

1 2 2 3 4
R

Cmaj13♯11

2 1 3 1 1
R

Cmaj13♯11

1 2 4 3
R

Minor Thirteenth (m13, min13, -13)

Cm13

2 3 3 4 4
R

Cm13

2 1 3 3 4
R

Cm13

1 3 1 2 4
R

Cm13
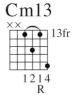
1 2 1 4
R

Minor 13th Chords with Alterations

Cm13♭5

1 2 1 1 4 1
R

Cm13♭5

1 2 1 3 4
R

Cm13♭5

3 4 2 1

Cm13♭5
3 4 1 2 1
R

C

Sixth Chords

Sixth Chords (6)

C6 · 2 143 · R · 7fr

C6 · 4231 · R

C6 · 13333 · R

C6 · 3241 · R · 8fr

Six-Nine Chords ($^6_9$)

C^6_9 · 21134 · R

C^6_9 · 2 1134 · R · 7fr

C^6_9 · 2134 · R · 9fr

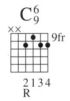

C^6_9 · 2113 · R

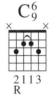

Minor Sixth Chords (m6)

Cm6 · 2 134 · R · 7fr

Cm6 · 3121 · R

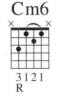

Cm6 · 3141 · R · 8fr

Cm6 · 1312 · R · 10fr

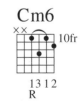

C

Minor Six-Nine Chords (m$_9^6$)

Cm$_9^6$
7fr
2 1334
R

Cm$_9^6$
31244
R

Cm$_9^6$
10fr
4311

Cm$_9^6$
8fr
2134
R

Power Chords ("5" Chords)

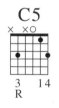

C5
3 14
R

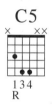

C5
134
R

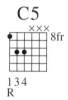

C5
8fr
134
R

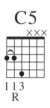

C5
113
R

Suspended (sus) and add Chords

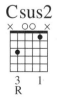

Csus2
3 1
R

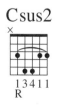

Csus2
13411
R

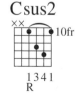

Csus2
10fr
1341
R

Csus2
7fr
2 134
R

C

Csus4

×   O   ×

3 4   1
R

Csus4

×   ×   3fr

1 3 3 4
R

Csus4

8fr

1 2 3 4 1 1
R

Csus4

× ×   10fr

1 3 4 4
R

Csus$_4^2$

×   × O

3   4 1
R

Csus$_4^2$

×   ×   5fr

4   1 3 2
R

Csus$_4^2$

× ×   8fr

2 3 1 4
R

Csus$_4^2$

×

1 1 4 1 1
R

C7sus4

×   3fr

1 3 1 4 1
R

C7sus4

8fr

1 3 1 4 1 1
R

C7sus4

× ×   10fr

1 3 2 4
R

C7sus4

×   ×

2 3 4 1
R

C

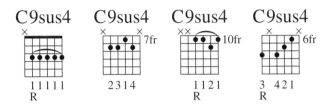

C9sus4
×
1 1 1 1 1
R

C9sus4
× 7fr
2 3 1 4

C9sus4
× × 10fr
1 1 2 1
R

C9sus4
× × 6fr
3 4 2 1
R

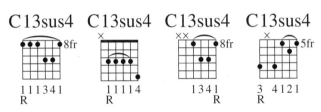

C13sus4
8fr
1 1 1 3 4 1
R

C13sus4
×
1 1 1 1 4
R

C13sus4
× × 8fr
1 3 4 1
R

C13sus4
× 5fr
3 4 1 2 1
R

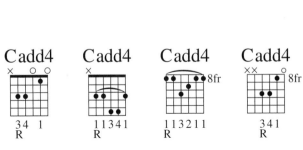

Cadd4
× O O
3 4 1
R

Cadd4
×
1 1 3 4 1
R

Cadd4
8fr
1 1 3 2 1 1
R

Cadd4
× × O 8fr
3 4 1
R

C

Cadd9

2 1 3 4
R

Cadd9
8fr
3 2 1 4
R

Cadd9
3fr
1 2 4 3 1
R

Cadd9

1 3 4 2
R

Cm(add9)

2 1 3 4
R

Cm(add9)
8fr
3 1 1 4
R

Cm(add9)
3fr
1 3 4 2 1
R

Cm(add9)
10fr
3 2 4 1
R

"No Third" Chords

C7(no 3rd)

R

C7(no 3rd)
8fr
2 3 4
R

C9(no 3rd)

2 3 3 3
R

C13(no 3rd)

1 2 2 4
R

C

Other Altered Chords

C(♭5)

1 2 3 4
R

C(♭5)

10fr

1 2 4 3
R

C(♭6)

3 2 1 1 4
R

C(♭6)

8fr

1 4 3 2 1 1
R

Open Voice Triads

C

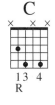

1 3 4
R

C

5fr

3 1 4
R

Cm

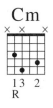

1 3 2
R

Cm

5fr

2 1 4
R

C°

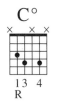

1 3 4
R

C°

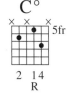

5fr

2 1 4
R

C+

3fr

1 4 3
R

C+

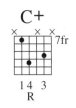

7fr

1 4 3
R

C#/Db

Triads

Major

Db   4fr

1 3 3 3 1
R

Db   9fr

1 3 4 2 1 1
R

Db

4 3 1 2 1
R

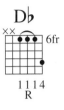

Db   6fr

1 1 1 4
R

Minor (m, -)

Dbm   4fr

1 3 4 2 1
R

Dbm   9fr

1 3 4 1 1 1
R

Dbm   11fr

1 3 4 2
R

Dbm   4fr

3 2 1
R

Diminished (°, dim)

Db°   8fr

2 1 3
R

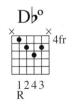

Db°   4fr

1 2 4 3
R

Db°

2
R

Db°   9fr

1 3 4 2
R

C#/D♭

Augmented (+, aug)

D♭+
×   2fr
3 2 1 1
R

D♭+
× ×   5fr
4 2 3 1
R

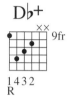

D♭+
× ×   9fr
1 4 3 2
R

D♭+
× × ×
2 3 1

Seventh Chords
Dominant Seventh (7)

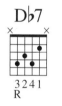

D♭7
×   ×
3 2 4 1
R

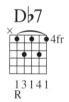

D♭7
×   4fr
1 3 1 4 1
R

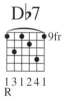

D♭7
   9fr
1 3 1 2 4 1
R

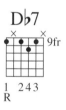

D♭7
×   ×   9fr
1   2 4 3
R

Dominant Seventh Chords with Alterations

D♭7♭5
×   8fr
2   3 4 1
R

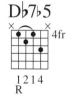

D♭7♭5
×   ×   4fr
1 2 1 4
R

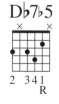

D♭7♭5
×   ×
2   3 4 1
R

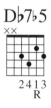

D♭7♭5
× ×
2 4 1 3
R

C#/D♭

D♭7#5

1 2 3 4
R

D♭7#5

1 2 4 3
R

D♭7#5

4 2 3 1
R

D♭7#5

2 1 1 3
R

D♭7♭9

2 1 3 1
R

D♭7♭9

1 3 2 4

D♭7♭9

2 1 3 1

D♭7♭9

1 3 2 4

D♭7#9

2 1 3 4
R

D♭7#9

1 3 3 3

D♭7#9

2 1 3 4
R

D♭7#9

1 2 1 4

C#/Db

$Db7^{b9}_{b5}$

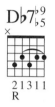

2 1 3 1 1
R

$Db7^{b9}_{b5}$

7fr

3 4 1 2

$Db7^{b9}_{b5}$

8fr

T 2 3 1 4
R

$Db7^{b9}_{b5}$

5fr

1 3 2 4

$Db7^{b9}_{\#5}$

2 1 3 1 4
R

$Db7^{b9}_{\#5}$

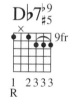

9fr

1 2 3 3 3
R

$Db7^{b9}_{\#5}$

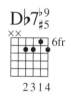

6fr

2 3 1 4

$Db7^{b9}_{\#5}$

7fr

3 2 1 1 4 1
R

$Db7^{\#9}_{\#11}$

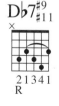

2 1 3 4 1
R

$Db7^{\#9}_{\#11}$

8fr

2 1 3 4 1
R

$Db7^{\#9}_{\#11}$

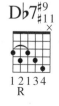

1 2 1 3 4
R

$Db7^{\#9}_{\#11}$

11fr

3 1 2 2 2
R

C#/D♭

Db7#9#5

2 1 3 4 4
R

Db7#9#5

8fr

2 1 3 3 4
R

Db7#9#5

8fr

1 2 2 4 3
R

Db7#9#5

1 2 3 4

Major Seventh (maj7, M7, ma7, △7)

Dbmaj7

4fr

1 3 2 4 1
R

Dbmaj7

9fr

1 3 4 2
R

Dbmaj7

4 3 1 1 1
R

Dbmaj7

6fr

1 1 1 3
R

Major Seventh Chords with Alterations

Dbmaj7b5

8fr

2 4 3 1 1
R

Dbmaj7b5

4fr

1 2 3 4
R

Dbmaj7b5

5fr

1 2 2 4
R

Dbmaj7b5

11fr

1 2 3 3
R

C#/D♭

D♭maj7#5

2 333
R

D♭maj7#5

1423
R

D♭maj7#5

2114
R

D♭maj7#5

43211
R

D♭maj7$^{#9}_{#11}$

21341
R

D♭maj7$^{#9}_{#11}$

21431
R

D♭maj7$^{#9}_{#11}$

1341
R

D♭maj7$^{#9}_{#11}$

1 423

Minor Seventh (m7, min7, -7)

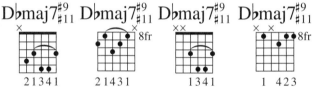

D♭m7

13121
R

D♭m7

131111
R

D♭m7

1314
R

D♭m7

1111
R

C#/Db

Minor Seventh Chords with Alterations

Dbm7b5

1 3 2 4
R

Dbm7b5

8fr
2 3 4 1
R

Dbm7b5

1 3 1 2
R

Dbm7b5

8fr
2 3 1 4
R

Minor-Major Seventh [m(maj7), m/M7]

Dbm(maj7)

1 4 2 3 1
R

Dbm(maj7)

9fr
1 3 2 1 1 1
R

Dbm(maj7)

9fr
1 4 2 3
R

Dbm(maj7)

1 4 1 3
R

Diminished Seventh (°7)

Db°7

3fr
2 3 1 4
R

Db°7

5fr
1 3 2 4
R

Db°7

8fr
2 1 3 1
R

Db°7

9fr
2 1 4 1
R

Ninth Chords C#/D♭

Dominant Ninth (9)

D♭9
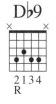

2 1 3 4
R

D♭9

8fr

1 3 2 4

D♭9

1 3 3 3

D♭9

10fr

2 1 4 3
R

Dominant Ninth Chords with Alterations

D♭9♭5
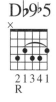

2 1 3 4 1
R

D♭9♭5

8fr

1 2 1 1

D♭9♭5

1 3 4 2

D♭9♭5

8fr

2 3 1 4

D♭9♯5
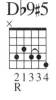

2 1 3 3 4
R

D♭9♯5

9fr

1 2 3 3 4
R

D♭9♯5

8fr

1 2 1 4

D♭9♯5

10fr

1 2 1 3 4
R

C#/Db

Major Ninth (maj9, M9, ma9, △9)

Dbmaj9

2 1 4 3
R

Dbmaj9

8fr
2 1 3 1 4
R

Dbmaj9

4 1 1 1 1
R

Dbmaj9

9fr
2 3 1 4

Minor Ninth (m9, min9, -9)

Dbm9

2 1 3 4
R

Dbm9

9fr
1 3 1 1 1 4
R

Dbm9

9fr
4 1 3 1
R

Dbm9

9fr
2 1 4 3
R

Minor Ninth Chords with Alterations

Dbm9b5

7fr
1 3 2 2 4
R

Dbm9b5

9fr
1 2 1 1 4 3
R

Dbm9b5

1 3 4 2

Dbm9b5

2

C#/D♭

Minor-Major Ninth [m(maj9), m/M9]

D♭m(maj9)   D♭m(maj9)   D♭m(maj9)   D♭m(maj9)

Eleventh Chords

Dominant Eleventh (11)

D♭11   D♭11   D♭11   D♭11

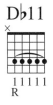
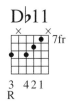
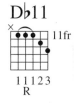

Major Eleventh (maj11, M11, ma11, △11)

D♭maj11   D♭maj11   D♭maj11   D♭maj11

C#/Db

Minor Eleventh (m11, min11, -11)

Dbm11

2 1 3 4 1
R

Dbm11

11fr
1 1 1 3 3
R

Dbm11

1 1 1 2 1
R

Dbm11

7fr
2 3 4 1
R

Thirteenth Chords

Dominant Thirteenth (13)

Db13

9fr
1 2 3 4
R

Db13

3fr
2 1 3 3 4
R

Db13

9fr
1 2 3 1
R

Db13

6fr
3 4 2 1 1
R

Dominant 13th Chords with Alterations

Db13#11

4fr
1 2 1 3 4
R

Db13#11

9fr
2 1 3 4

Db13#11

6fr
3 4 2 1

Db13#11

4fr
2 1 3 4

C#/D♭

D♭13♭9

3 4211
R

D♭13♭9

1214

D♭13♭9

1243

D♭13♭9

1333

D♭13#9

1234

D♭13#9

21334
R

D♭13#9

1234

D♭13#9

1224

Major Thirteenth (maj13, M13, ma13, △13)

D♭maj13

1 234
R

D♭maj13

3 4211
R

D♭maj13

1 234
R

D♭maj13

2341
R

C#/D♭

Major 13th Chords with Alterations

D♭maj13#11 D♭maj13#11 D♭maj13#11 D♭maj13#11

1 2 2 3 4
R

1 2 2 3 4
R

2 1 3 1 1
R

2 4 1 3 1

Minor Thirteenth (m13, min13, -13)

D♭m13   D♭m13   D♭m13   D♭m13

2 3 3 4
R

1 3 1 1 4 1
R

1 3 1 2 4
R

1 1 3 4

Minor 13th Chords with Alterations

D♭m13♭5   D♭m13♭5   D♭m13♭5   D♭m13♭5

1 2 1 1 4 1
R

1 2 1 3 4
R

3 4 2 1

2 1 3 4

C#/D♭

Sixth Chords

Sixth Chords (6)

Db6

8fr
2 143
R

Db6
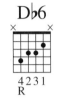
4231
R

Db6
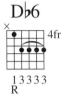
4fr
13333
R

Db6
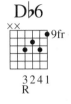
9fr
3241
R

Six-Nine Chords ($^6_9$)

Db$^6_9$

21134
R

Db$^6_9$

8fr
2 1134
R

Db$^6_9$
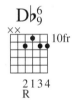
10fr
2134
R

Db$^6_9$
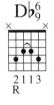
2113
R

Minor Sixth Chords (m6)

Dbm6

8fr
2 134
R

Dbm6
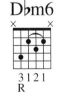
3121
R

Dbm6

9fr
3141
R

Dbm6

8fr
2 13
R

C#/D♭

Minor Six-Nine Chords (m⁶₉)

$D\flat m_9^6$

3124
R

$D\flat m_9^6$

8fr

3 124
R

$D\flat m_9^6$

9fr

2134
R

$D\flat m_9^6$
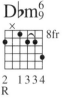

8fr

2 1334
R

Power Chords ("5" Chords)

$D\flat 5$

4fr

134
R

$D\flat 5$

9fr

134
R

$D\flat 5$

11
R

$D\flat 5$
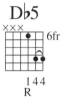

6fr

144
R

Suspended (sus) and add Chords

$D\flat sus2$

4fr

13411
R

$D\flat sus2$

11fr

1341
R

$D\flat sus2$

8fr

2 134
R

$D\flat sus2$

4112
R

C#/D♭

D♭sus4

1 3 3 4
R

D♭sus4

1 2 3 4 1 1
R

D♭sus4

1 3 4 4
R

D♭sus4

3 4 1 2
R

D♭sus$_4^2$

3   4 1
R

D♭sus$_4^2$

4   1 3 2
R

D♭sus$_4^2$

2 3 1 4
R

D♭sus$_4^2$

1 1 4 1 1
R

D♭7sus4

1 3 1 4 1
R

D♭7sus4

1 3 1 4 1 1
R

D♭7sus4

1 3 2 4
R

D♭7sus4

2 2 3 1 4
R

C#/D♭

D♭9sus4

1 1 1 1 1
R

D♭9sus4

7fr

3 2 1 4
R

D♭9sus4

11fr

1 1 2 1
R

D♭9sus4

7fr

3 4 2 1
R

D♭13sus4

9fr

1 2 1 3 4 1
R

D♭13sus4

4fr

1 1 1 1 4
R

D♭13sus4

9fr

1 3 4 2
R

D♭13sus4

6fr

4 1 2 1
R

D♭add4

3 4 1 2 1
R

D♭add4

4fr

1 1 3 4 1
R

D♭add4

9fr

1 1 3 2 1 1
R

D♭add4

7fr

2 4 3 1
R

C#/D♭

D♭add9

× × ×
3 2 1 4
R

D♭add9

× ×　9fr
3 2 1 4
R

D♭add9

9fr
1 3 4 2 1 1

D♭add9

× ×　6fr
1 3 1 4
R

D♭m(add9)

× ×
3 2 1 4
R

D♭m(add9)

× ×　9fr
3 1 1 4
R

D♭m(add9)

9fr
1 3 4 1 1 1
R

D♭m(add9)

× ×　11fr
3 2 4 1
R

"No Third" Chords

D♭7(no 3rd)
× ×　4fr
1 3 1
R

D♭7(no 3rd)
× ×　2fr
2　3 1 4
R

D♭9(no 3rd)
×　4fr
1 3 1 1 1
R

D♭13(no 3rd)
×　4fr
1 3 1 1 4
R

C#/Db

Other Altered Chords

Db(b5)

4fr
1 2 3 4
R

Db(b5)

11fr
1 2 4 3
R

Db(b6)

3 2 1 1 4
R

Db(b6)
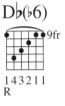
9fr
1 4 3 2 1 1
R

Open Voice Triads

Db

3fr
2 1 4
R

Db

6fr
3 1 4
R

Dbm

2fr
2 1 4
R

Dbm
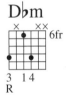
6fr
3 1 4
R

Db°

2fr
2 1 4
R

Db°
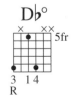
5fr
3 1 4
R

Db+

3fr
3 1 4
R

Db+
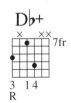
7fr
3 1 4
R

D

Triads

Major

D — × × ○ — 1 3 2 — R

D — × — 5fr — 1 3 3 3 1 — R

D — 10fr — 1 3 4 2 1 1 — R

D — × × — 7fr — 1 1 1 4 — R

Minor (m, -)

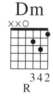

Dm — × — 5fr — 1 3 4 2 1 — R

Dm — 10fr — 1 3 4 1 1 1 — R

Dm — × × ○ — 3 4 2 — R

Dm — × × ○ — 5fr — 3 2 1 — R

Diminished (°, dim)

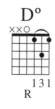

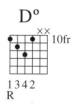

D° — × × × — 9fr — 2 1 3 — R

D° — × — × — 5fr — 1 2 4 3 — R

D° — × × ○ — 1 3 1 — R

D° — × × — 10fr — 1 3 4 2 — R

D

Augmented (+, aug)

D+
3211
R

D+
4231
R

D+
1432
R

D+
231
R

Seventh Chords
Dominant Seventh (7)

D7
3241
R

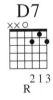

D7
13141
R

D7
213
R

D7
1 243

Dominant Seventh Chords with Alterations

D7♭5
2 341
R

D7♭5
1214
R

D7♭5
2 341
R

D7♭5
2413
R

D

D7#5

× × 10fr
1 2 3 4
R

D7#5

× × 5fr
1 2 4 3
R

D7#5

× 3fr
4 2 3 1
R

D7#5

× × 10fr
1 3 4 2
R

D7♭9

× ×
2 1 3 1
R

D7♭9

× × 10fr
1 2 3 4
R

D7♭9

× × 4fr
2 1 3 1

D7♭9

× × 5fr
2 3 1 4

D7#9

× × 4fr
2 1 3 4
R

D7#9

× × 9fr
1 3 3 3

D7#9

× × 11fr
2 1 3 4
R

D7#9

× × 10fr
1 2 1 4

D

$D7^{\flat 9}_{\flat 5}$

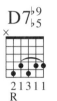

×
2 1 3 1 1
R

$D7^{\flat 9}_{\flat 5}$

× ×
1 3 2 4

$D7^{\flat 9}_{\flat 5}$

× 9fr
T 2 3 1 4
R

$D7^{\flat 9}_{\flat 5}$

× × 6fr
1 3 2 4

$D7^{\flat 9}_{\sharp 5}$

× 4fr
2 1 3 1 4
R

$D7^{\flat 9}_{\sharp 5}$

× 10fr
1 2 3 3 3
R

$D7^{\flat 9}_{\sharp 5}$

× × 7fr
2 3 1 4

$D7^{\flat 9}_{\sharp 5}$

× × 8fr
3 2 1 1 4
R

$D7^{\sharp 9}_{\sharp 11}$

× 4fr
2 1 3 4 1
R

$D7^{\sharp 9}_{\sharp 11}$

× 9fr
2 1 3 4 1
R

$D7^{\sharp 9}_{\sharp 11}$

× 11fr
1 2 1 3 4
R

$D7^{\sharp 9}_{\sharp 11}$

× ○
2   1 1 1
R

D

$D7^{\sharp 9}_{\sharp 5}$
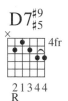
4fr

2 1 3 4 4
R

$D7^{\sharp 9}_{\sharp 5}$

9fr

2 1 3 3 4
R

$D7^{\sharp 9}_{\sharp 5}$

7fr

2 4 1 3

$D7^{\sharp 9}_{\sharp 5}$
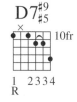
10fr

1 2 3 3 4
R

Major Seventh (maj7, M7, ma7, △7)

Dmaj7

1 1 1
R

Dmaj7
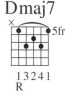
5fr

1 3 2 4 1
R

Dmaj7
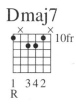
10fr

1 3 4 2
R

Dmaj7
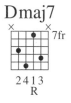
7fr

2 4 1 3
R

Major Seventh Chords with Alterations

Dmaj7♭5

9fr

2 4 3 1 1
R

Dmaj7♭5

5fr

1 2 3 4
R

Dmaj7♭5
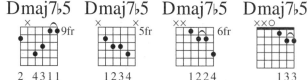
6fr

1 2 2 4
R

Dmaj7♭5

1 3 3
R

D

Dmaj7♯5

×   × ×
10fr

1 3 3 3
R

Dmaj7♯5

5fr

1 4 2 3
R

Dmaj7♯5

× ×
7fr

2 1 1 4
R

Dmaj7♯5

× × ○
6fr

2 1 1
R

Dmaj7$^{♯9}_{♯11}$

×
4fr

2 1 3 4 1
R

Dmaj7$^{♯9}_{♯11}$

× ×
9fr

2 1 4 3 1
R

Dmaj7$^{♯9}_{♯11}$

×
6fr

3 1 2 1 4
R

Dmaj7$^{♯9}_{♯11}$

×
9fr

1 4 2 3
R

Minor Seventh (m7, min7, -7)

Dm7

×
5fr

1 3 1 2 1
R

Dm7

10fr

1 3 1 1 1 1
R

Dm7

× ×
6fr

2 3 1 4
R

Dm7

× × ○
6fr

2 1 1
R

D

Minor Seventh Chords with Alterations

Dm7♭5   Dm7♭5   Dm7♭5   Dm7♭5

Minor-Major Seventh [m(maj7), m/M7]

Dm(maj7)   Dm(maj7)   Dm(maj7)   Dm(maj7)

Diminished Seventh (°7)

D°7   D°7 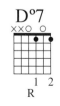 D°7   D°7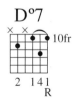

D

Ninth Chords

Dominant Ninth (9)

D9

2 1 3 4
R

D9

9fr

1 3 2 4 4
R

D9

3 4 1
R

D9

11fr

2 1 4 3
R

Dominant Ninth Chords with Alterations

D9♭5

2 1 3 4 1
R

D9♭5

9fr

2 1 3 1 1
R

D9♭5

9fr

1 2 1 4 3

D9♭5

9fr

2 3 1 4

D9♯5

4fr

2 1 3 3 4
R

D9♯5

10fr

1 2 3 3 4
R

D9♯5

9fr

1 2 1 4 3
R

D9♯5

10fr

1 2 3 4

D

Major Ninth (maj9, M9, ma9, △9)

Dmaj9

2 1 4 3
R

Dmaj9

4fr
2 1 4 1 3
R

Dmaj9

6fr
2 3
R

Dmaj9

10fr
2 3 1 4

Minor Ninth (m9, min9, -9)

Dm9

2 1 3 4
R

Dm9

10fr
1 3 1 1 1 4
R

Dm9

5fr
2 3
R

Dm9
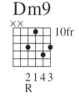
10fr
2 1 4 3
R

Minor Ninth Chords with Alterations

Dm9#11

8fr
1 3 2 2 4
R

Dm9#11
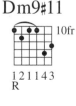
10fr
1 2 1 1 4 3
R

Dm9#11

5fr
1 3 2 4
R

Dm9#11
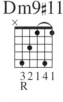
3 2 1 4 1
R

D

Minor-Major Ninth [m(maj9), m/M9]

Dm(maj9)

2 1 4 3
R

Dm(maj9)

1 3 2 1 1 4
R

Dm(maj9)

3 4
R

Dm(maj9)

2 1 4 3
R

Eleventh Chords

Dominant Eleventh (11)

D11

2   3 4 1
R

D11

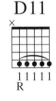

1 1 1 1 1
R

D11

3   4 2 1
R

D11

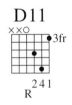

2 4 1
R

Major Eleventh (maj11, M11, ma11, △11)

Dmaj11

2   3 4 1
R

Dmaj11

1 1 2 3 1
R

Dmaj11

2   3 4 1
R

Dmaj11

3 4 1
R

D

Minor Eleventh (m11, min11, -11)

Dm11
×
2 1 3 4 1
R

Dm11
× × ○ 3fr
3 4 1
R

Dm11
× × 5fr
1 1 1 2 1
R

Dm11
× × 8fr
2 3 4 1

Thirteenth Chords

Dominant Thirteenth (13)

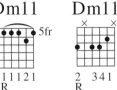

D13
× × 10fr
1 2 3 4
R

D13
× 4fr
2 1 3 3 4
R

D13
× × ○ 5fr
1 3 4
R

D13
× 7fr
3 4 2 1 1
R

Dominant 13th Chords with Alterations

D13♯11
× 5fr
1 2 1 3 4
R

D13♯11
× 10fr
2 1 3 4 1
R

D13♯11
× 7fr
2 4 2 3 1

D13♯11
× 10fr
4 1 3 2 1
R

D

D13♭9

× ⌒ 7fr

3 4211
R

D13♭9

× ⌒ 4fr

2131 4
R

D13♭9

×× 10fr

1243

D13♭9

× × ×

1333

D13♯9

× × 4fr

1234

D13♯9

× ⌒ 9fr

12334
R

D13♯9

× 10fr

T 1234
R

D13♯9

×× ⌒ 7fr

3411

Major Thirteenth (maj13, M13, ma13, △13)

Dmaj13

× × 10fr

1 234
R

Dmaj13

× ⌒ 7fr

3 4211
R

Dmaj13

× × 5fr

1 244
R

Dmaj13

××○ 6fr

234
R

D

Major 13th Chords with Alterations

Dmaj13#11　Dmaj13#11　Dmaj13#11　Dmaj13#11

12224　　12234　　211311　　22231
R　　　　R　　　　R　　　　　　R

Minor Thirteenth (m13, min13, -13)

Dm13　　　Dm13　　　Dm13　　　Dm13

2　334　　1131　　13124　　21334
R　　　　　　　R　　　R　　　　R

Minor 13th Chords with Alterations

Dm13♭5　　Dm13♭5　　Dm13♭5　　Dm13♭5

121141　　12134　　3421　　2134

D

Sixth Chords

Sixth Chords (6)

D6
× ×
9fr
2 1 4 3
R

D6
× × ○ ○
2 3
R

D6
×
5fr
1 3 3 3 3
R

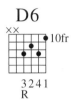

D6
× ×
10fr
3 2 4 1
R

Six-Nine Chords ($^6_9$)

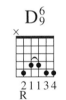

D$^6_9$
×
2 1 1 3 4
R

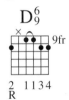

D$^6_9$
×
9fr
2 1 1 3 4
R

D$^6_9$
× ×
11fr
2 1 3 4

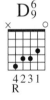

D$^6_9$
× ○
4 2 3 1
R

Minor Sixth Chords (m6)

Dm6
× ×
9fr
2 1 3 4
R

Dm6
× ×
3 1 2 1
R

Dm6
× × ○ ○
2 1
R

Dm6
× ×
4fr
2 4 1 3
R

D

Minor Six-Nine Chords (m$_9^6$)

Dm$_9^6$

× ×

3 1 2 4
R

Dm$_9^6$

× ○ 7fr

2 3 1 4
R

Dm$_9^6$

× × 10fr

2 1 3 4
R

Dm$_9^6$

× 9fr

2 1 3 3 4
R

Power Chords ("5" Chords)

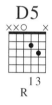

D5

× × ○ ×

1 3
R

D5

× × × 5fr

1 3 4
R

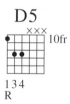

D5

× × × 10fr

1 3 4
R

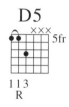

D5

× × × 5fr

1 1 3
R

Suspended (sus) and add Chords

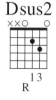

Dsus2

× × ○ ○

1 3
R

Dsus2

× 5fr

1 3 4 1 1
R

Dsus2

× × 7fr

1 3 4 4
R

Dsus2

× × 9fr

2 1 3 4
R

D

Dsus4

× × ○

1 3 4
R

Dsus4

×   × 5fr

1 3 3 4
R

Dsus4

× × ○ 5fr

3 4 1
R

Dsus4
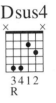
×   ×

3 4 1 2
R

Dsus$\frac{2}{4}$

× × ○ ○   ○

3
R

Dsus$\frac{2}{4}$
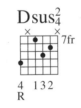
× 7fr

4   1 3 2
R

Dsus$\frac{2}{4}$
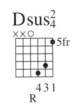
× × ○ 5fr

4 3 1
R

Dsus$\frac{2}{4}$

× 5fr

1 1 4 1 1
R

D7sus4

× × ○

2 1 4
R

D7sus4

10fr

1 3 1 4 1 1
R

D7sus4
× 5fr

1 3 1 4 1
R

D7sus4
× × 7fr

1 1 3 3
R

D

D9sus4

×

1 1 1 1 1
R

D9sus4

×× 9fr

3 2 1 4
R

D9sus4

×× ○○ ○

1
R

D9sus4
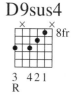

× × 8fr

3 4 2 1
R

D13sus4
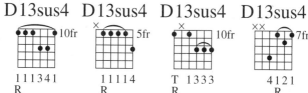

10fr

1 1 1 3 4 1
R

D13sus4

× 5fr

1 1 1 1 4
R

D13sus4
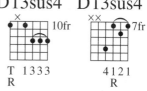

× 10fr

T 1 3 3 3
R

D13sus4

×× 7fr

4 1 2 1
R

Dadd4
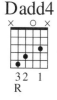

× ○ ×

3 2 1
R

Dadd4
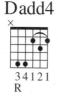

×

3 4 1 2 1
R

Dadd4

×× ○○

3 2
R

Dadd4

10fr

1 1 3 2 1 1
R

D

Dadd9

1 4 1
R

Dadd9

10fr
3 2 1 4
R

Dadd9

7fr
3 4
R

Dadd9

7fr
2 1 3 4 4
R

Dm(add9)

3 2 1 4
R

Dm(add9)
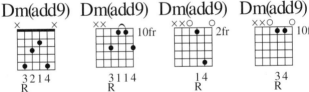
10fr
3 1 1 4
R

Dm(add9)

2fr
1 4
R

Dm(add9)
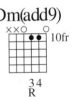
10fr
3 4
R

"No Third" Chords

D7(no 3rd)

2 1
R

D7(no 3rd)

7fr
1 4 2
R

D9(no 3rd)

9fr
2 3 1 4
R

D13(no 3rd)

7fr
3 1 4 1
R

D

Other Altered Chords

D(♭5)

1 2 3 4
R

D(♭5)
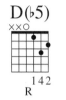
1 4 2
R

D(♭6)

3 2 1 1 4
R

D(♭6)
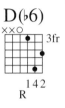
1 4 2
R

Open Voice Triads

D

2 1 4
R

D

3 1 4
R

Dm

2 1 4
R

Dm

3 1 4
R

D°

2 1 4
R

D°

3 1 4
R

D+

3 1 4
R

D+

3 1 4
R

D#/E♭

Triads

Major

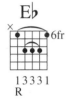
Eb
×   ●6fr
1 3 3 3 1
R

Eb
●11fr
1 3 4 2 1 1
R

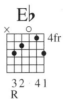
Eb
×   ○
4fr
3 2   4 1
R

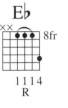
Eb
× ×
8fr
1 1 1 4
R

Minor (m, -)

Ebm
×
●6fr
1 3 4 2 1
R

Ebm
●11fr
1 3 4 1 1 1
R

Ebm
× ×
1 3 4 2
R

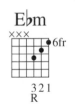
Ebm
× × ×
●6fr
3 2 1
R

Diminished (°, dim)

Eb°
×   ×
6fr
1 2 4 3
R

Eb°
× × ×
10fr
2 1 3
R

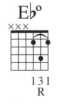
Eb°
× × ×
1 3 1
R

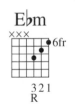
Eb°
× ×
11fr
1 3 4 2
R

D#/E♭

Augmented (+, aug)

Eb+
× ×
3 2 1 1
R
4fr

Eb+
× ×
4 2 3 1
R
7fr

Eb+
× ×
1 4 3 2
R
3fr

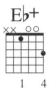

Eb+
× × ○ ○
1   4

Seventh Chords
Dominant Seventh (7)

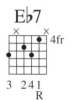

Eb7
×   ×
3 2 4 1
R
4fr

Eb7
×
1 3 1 4 1
R
6fr

Eb7
× ×
1 2 1 1
R
11fr

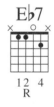

Eb7
×   ○   ×
1 2   4
R

Dominant Seventh Chords with Alterations

Eb7b5
×   ×
2   3 4 1
R
10fr

Eb7b5
×   ×
1 2 1 4
R
6fr

Eb7b5
×   ×
2   3 4 1
R
4fr

Eb7b5
× ×
1 2 3 4
R

D#/E♭

E♭7#5

1 2 3 4
R

E♭7#5

1 3 4 2
R

E♭7#5

4 2 3 1
R

E♭7#5
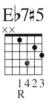

1 4 2 3
R

E♭7♭9

2 1 3 1
R

E♭7♭9

1 3 2 4

E♭7♭9

2 1 3 1
R

E♭7♭9
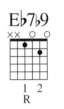

1 2
R

E♭7#9

2 1 3 4
R

E♭7#9

1 3 3 3

E♭7#9
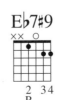

2 3 4
R

E♭7#9
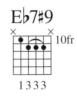

T T 1 2 4 3
R

D♯/E♭

E♭7♭9♭5
×
5fr
2 1 3 1 1
R

E♭7♭9♭5
×   ○
6fr
1 2 1 4
R

E♭7♭9♭5
×
10fr
T 2 3 1 4
R

E♭7♭9♭5
× ×
7fr
1 3 2 4

E♭7♭9♯5
×
5fr
2 1 3 1 4
R

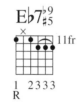

E♭7♭9♯5
×
11fr
1 2 3 3 3
R

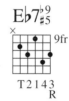

E♭7♭9♯5
×
9fr
T 2 1 4 3
R

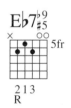

E♭7♭9♯5
×   ○ ○
5fr
2 1 3
R

E♭7♯9♯11
×
5fr
2 1 3 4 1
R

E♭7♯9♯11
×   ×
10fr
2 1 3 4 1
R

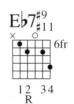

E♭7♯9♯11
×   ○
6fr
1 2 3 4
R

E♭7♯9♯11
×
5fr
4 1 2 2 3
R

D♯/E♭

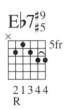

Eb7#9#5
5fr
× ●●●○
2 1 3 4 4
R

Eb7#9#5
10fr
2 1 3 3 4
R

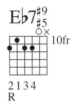

Eb7#9#5
10fr
2 1 3 4
R

Eb7#9#5
3 1 4 2 2
R

Major Seventh (maj7, M7, ma7, △7)

Ebmaj7
6fr
1 3 2 4 1
R

Ebmaj7
11fr
1   3 4 2
R

Ebmaj7
3fr
4 3 1 1
R

Ebmaj7
1 2   4
R

Major Seventh Chords with Alterations

Ebmaj7b5
10fr
2   3 4 1
R

Ebmaj7b5
3   1 2 4
R

Ebmaj7b5
7fr
1 2 2 4
R

Ebmaj7b5
1 2 3 3
R

D#/E♭

Ebmaj7#5

×   ×
11fr

1 333
R

Ebmaj7#5

21 4
R

Ebmaj7#5

× ×
8fr

2114
R

Ebmaj7#5

×   ×

2 143
R

Ebmaj7#9#11

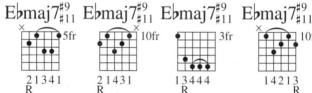

×   5fr

21341
R

Ebmaj7#9#11

×   ×
10fr

2 1431
R

Ebmaj7#9#11

3fr

13444
R

Ebmaj7#9#11

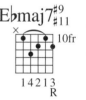

×
10fr

14213
      R

Minor Seventh (m7, min7, -7)

Ebm7

×   ×
6fr

13121
R

Ebm7

×   ×
4fr

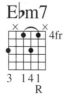

3 141
  R

Ebm7

× ×
7fr

2314
R

Ebm7

×   ×
11fr

2 333
R

D♯/E♭

Minor Seventh Chords with Alterations

E♭m7♭5
1 3 2 4
R

E♭m7♭5
2   3 4 1
R

E♭m7♭5
2 1 4 1
R

E♭m7♭5
1 2 1 4
R

Minor-Major Seventh [m(maj7), m/M7]

E♭m(maj7)
1 4 2 3 1
R

E♭m(maj7)
1 3 4 2
R

E♭m(maj7)
1   4 2 3
R

E♭m(maj7)
2   1 3 4
R

Diminished Seventh (°7)

E♭°7
2 3 1 4
R

E♭°7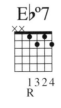
1 3 2 4
R

E♭°7
2   1 3 1
R

E♭°7
2   1 4 1
R

Ninth Chords D#/E♭

Dominant Ninth (9)

Eb9

Eb9

Eb9

Eb9

Dominant Ninth Chords with Alterations

Eb9b5

Eb9b5

Eb9b5

Eb9b5

Eb9#5

Eb9#5

Eb9#5

Eb9#5

D#/E♭

Major Ninth (maj9, M9, ma9, △9)

E♭maj9

2 1 4 3
R

E♭maj9
5fr

2 1 4 1 3
R

E♭maj9

3fr

4 1 1 1 1
R

E♭maj9

11fr

1 2 3 4
R

Minor Ninth (m9, min9, -9)

E♭m9

4fr

2 1 3 4
R

E♭m9

11fr

1 3 1 1 1 4
R

E♭m9

11fr

4 1 3 1
R

E♭m9

11fr

2 1 4 3
R

Minor Ninth Chords with Alterations

E♭m9♭5

9fr

1 3 2 2 4
R

E♭m9♭5

11fr

1 2 1 1 4 3
R

E♭m9♭5

4fr

T 2 1 3 4
R

E♭m9♭5

2fr

2 1 1 1

D#/E♭

Minor-Major Ninth [m(maj9), m/M9]

E♭m(maj9)   E♭m(maj9)   E♭m(maj9)   E♭m(maj9)

2 1 4 3   1 3 2 1 1 4   1 4 2 3   2 1 4 3
R   R   R

Eleventh Chords

Dominant Eleventh (11)

E♭11   E♭11   E♭11   E♭11

2   3 4 1   1 1 1 1 1   3   4 2 1   1 1 1 2 3
R   R   R   R

Major Eleventh (maj11, M11, ma11, △11)

E♭maj11   E♭maj11   E♭maj11   E♭maj11

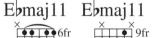

2   4 3 1   1 1 2 1 1   3   4 2 1   1 1 1 3 3
R   R   R   R

D#/Eb

Minor Eleventh (m11, min11, -11)

Ebm11

Ebm11

Ebm11

Ebm11

Thirteenth Chords

Dominant Thirteenth (13)

Eb13

Eb13

Eb13

Eb13

Dominant 13th Chords with Alterations

Eb13#11

Eb13#11

Eb13#11

Eb13#11

D#/E♭

E♭13♭9

×

8fr

3 4211
R

E♭13♭9

×

5fr

21314
R

E♭13♭9

× ×

11fr

1243

E♭13♭9

×   ×

1333

E♭13#9

× ×

5fr

1234

E♭13#9

×

10fr

12243
R

E♭13#9

×

11fr

T 1234
R

E♭13#9

×   ×

4fr

1224

Major Thirteenth (maj13, M13, ma13, △13)

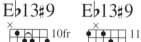

E♭maj13
×

11fr

1 234
R

E♭maj13

×

8fr

3 4211
R

E♭maj13

× ×

6fr

1   234
R

E♭maj13
× ×

11fr

2341
R

D#/E♭

Major 13th Chords with Alterations

E♭maj13#11 E♭maj13#11 E♭maj13#11 E♭maj13#11

12224
R

12244
R

2 1311
R

12 34
R

Minor Thirteenth (m13, min13, -13)

E♭m13   E♭m13   E♭m13   E♭m13

2 3344
R

131141
R

13124
R

23141

Minor 13th Chords with Alterations

E♭m13♭5 E♭m13♭5 E♭m13♭5 E♭m13♭5

121141
R

12134
R

3421

2 1333

D#/E♭

Sixth Chords

Sixth Chords (6)

Eb6
×　　×　　10fr
2　143
R

Eb6
×　×
1314
R

Eb6
×　　　　8fr
4　1111
R

Eb6
××　　　11fr
3241
R

Six-Nine Chords (⁶₉)

Eb⁶₉
×　　　5fr
21134
R

Eb⁶₉
×　　　10fr
2　1134
R

Eb⁶₉
××　　○
1　23
R

Eb⁶₉
×　　　10fr
11133
R

Minor Sixth Chords (m6)

Ebm6
×　　×　　10fr
2　134
R

Ebm6
×　×　　4fr
3121
R

Ebm6
××　　　11fr
3141

Ebm6
××
1312
R

D#/Eb

Minor Six-Nine Chords (m⁶₉)

Ebm⁶₉
× 4fr
3 1 2 4
R

Ebm⁶₉
× × 11fr
4 1 2 1
R

Ebm⁶₉
× × 11fr
2 1 3 4
R

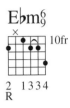
Ebm⁶₉
× 10fr
2 1 3 3 4
R

Power Chords ("5" Chords)

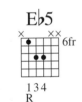
Eb5
× × × 6fr
1 3 4
R

Eb5
× × × 11fr
1 3 4
R

Eb5
× × × 6fr
1 1 3
R

Eb5
× × ×
1 3 4
R

Suspended (sus) and add Chords

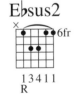
Ebsus2
× 6fr
1 3 4 1 1
R

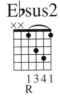
Ebsus2
× ×
1 3 4 1
R

Ebsus2
× × 10fr
2 1 3 4
R

Ebsus2
× 3fr
4 1 1 2
R

D♯/E♭

E♭sus4

6fr

1 3 3 4
R

E♭sus4
11fr

1 2 3 4 1 1
R

E♭sus4

1 3 4 4
R

E♭sus4

3fr

3 4 1 2
R

E♭sus$_4^2$

3fr

3 2 4 1
R

E♭sus$_4^2$

8fr

4 1 3 2
R

E♭sus$_4^2$

11fr

2 3 1 4
R

E♭sus$_4^2$

6fr

1 1 4 1 1
R

E♭7sus4

6fr

1 3 1 4 1
R

E♭7sus4

11fr

1 3 1 4 1 1
R

E♭7sus4

1 3 2 4
R

E♭7sus4

8fr

1 1 3 3
R

D#/E♭

E♭9sus4

× ●●●●● 6fr

1 1 1 1 1
R

E♭9sus4

× 10fr

2 3 1 4

E♭9sus4

× ×

1 1 2 1
R

E♭9sus4

× × ● 9fr

3 2 1 4
R

E♭13sus4

● ● ● ● 11fr

1 1 1 3 4 1
R

E♭13sus4

× 6fr

1 1 1 1 4
R

E♭13sus4

× × ● 11fr

1 3 4 2
R

E♭13sus4

× 8fr

3 4 1 2 1
R

E♭add4

× ● 3fr

3 4 1 2 1
R

E♭add4

× ● 6fr

1 1 3 4 1
R

E♭add4

× × 11fr

1 1 3 2 1 1
R

E♭add4

× × ○

1 4 4
R

D♯/E♭

E♭add9

×   ×   3fr

3 2 1 4
R

E♭add9
11fr

3 2 1 4
R

E♭add9

8fr

1 3 1 4
    R

E♭add9

11fr

1   3 2 4
R

E♭m(add9)

3fr

3 2 1 4
R

E♭m(add9)
11fr

3 1 1 4
R

E♭m(add9)

6fr

1 3 4 2 1
R

E♭m(add9)

3 2 4 1
    R

"No Third" Chords

E♭7(no 3rd)   E♭7(no 3rd) E♭9(no 3rd) E♭13(no 3rd)

1 1 3 2   2   1 3   1 3 2 1   1 3 1 1 4
   R   R   R   R

D♯/E♭

Other Altered Chords

E♭(♭5)

×   ×   6fr

1 2 3 4
R   R

E♭(♭5)

× ×

1 2 4 3
R   R

E♭(♭6)

×   4fr

3 2 1 1 4
R   R

E♭(♭6)

11fr

1 4 3 2 1 1
R   R

Open Voice Triads

E♭

×   × ×
5fr

2   1 4
   R

E♭

×   × ×
8fr

3   1 4
R

E♭m

×   × ×
4fr

2   1 4
    R

E♭m

×   × ×
8fr

3   1 4
R

E♭°

×   × ×
4fr

2   1 4
   R

E♭°

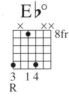

×   × ×
8fr

3   1 4
R

E♭+

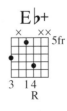

×   × ×
5fr

3   1 4
   R

E♭+

×   × ×
9fr

3   1 4
R

E

Triads

Major

E

E

E

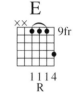
E

Minor (m, -)

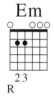
Em

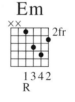
Em

Em

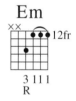
Em

Diminished (°, dim)

E°

E°

E°

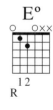
E°

E

Augmented (+, aug)

E+

3 2 1 1
R

E+

4 2 3 1
R

E+

1 4 3 2
R

E+

2 3 1
R

Seventh Chords
Dominant Seventh (7)

E7

2   1
R

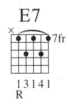

E7

1 3 1 4 1
R

E7

3 2 4 1
R

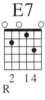

E7

2   1 4
R

Dominant Seventh Chords with Alterations

E7♭5

2 3 4 1
R

E7♭5

1 2 1 4
R

E7♭5

2 3 4 1
R

E7♭5

1 2 3 4
R

E

E7#5

1 2 3 4
R

E7#5

1 2 4 3
R

E7#5

4 2 3 1
R

E7#5

2 3
R

E7♭9

2 1 3 1
R

E7♭9

T 1 3 2 4
R

E7♭9

2 1 3 1
R

E7♭9

1 3 2 4

E7#9

2 1 3 4
R

E7#9

1 3 3 3
R

E7#9

2 1 4 4
R

E7#9

1 2 4 3

E

$E7^{\flat 9}_{\flat 5}$

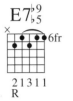

2 1 3 1 1
R

$E7^{\flat 9}_{\flat 5}$

1 2 1 3 1

$E7^{\flat 9}_{\flat 5}$

T 2 3 1 4
R

$E7^{\flat 9}_{\flat 5}$

1 3 2 4

$E7^{\flat 9}_{\sharp 5}$

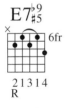

2 1 3 1 4
R

$E7^{\flat 9}_{\sharp 5}$

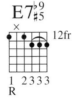

1 2 3 3 3
R

$E7^{\flat 9}_{\sharp 5}$

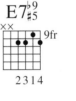

2 3 1 4

$E7^{\flat 9}_{\sharp 5}$

4 2 1 3 1
R

$E7^{\sharp 9}_{\sharp 11}$

2 1 3 4 1
R

$E7^{\sharp 9}_{\sharp 11}$

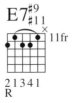

2 1 3 4 1
R

$E7^{\sharp 9}_{\sharp 11}$

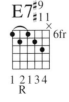

1 2 1 3 4
R

$E7^{\sharp 9}_{\sharp 11}$

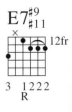

3 1 2 2 2
R

E

$E7^{\sharp9}_{\sharp5}$

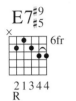

×   6fr

2 1 3 4 4
R

$E7^{\sharp9}_{\sharp5}$

× 11fr

2 1 3 3 4
R

$E7^{\sharp9}_{\sharp5}$

×   o   9fr

2   3 4 1
R

$E7^{\sharp9}_{\sharp5}$

× ×   6fr

3   1 2 4

Major Seventh (maj7, M7, ma7, △7)

Emaj7

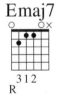

o   o ×

3 1 2
R

Emaj7

×   7fr

1 3 2 4 1
R

Emaj7

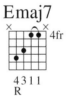

×   × 4fr

4 3 1 1
R

Emaj7

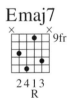

×   × 9fr

2 4 1 3
R

Major Seventh Chords with Alterations

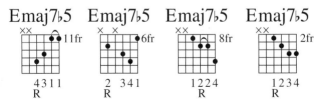

Emaj7♭5

× ×　11fr

4 3 1 1
R

Emaj7♭5

× × 6fr

2   3 4 1
R

Emaj7♭5

× × 8fr

1 2 2 4
R

Emaj7♭5

× × 2fr

1 2 3 4
R

E

Emaj7#5

1 1 1
R

Emaj7#5

7fr
1 4 2 3
R

Emaj7#5

9fr
2 1 1 4
R

Emaj7#5

4fr
4 3 2 1 1
R

Emaj7$^{#9}_{#11}$

6fr
2 1 3 4 1
R

Emaj7$^{#9}_{#11}$

T 1 2 4 3

Emaj7$^{#9}_{#11}$
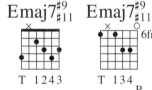
6fr
T 1 3 4
R

Emaj7$^{#9}_{#11}$

11fr
1 4 2 3

Minor Seventh (m7, min7, -7)

Em7

2 3
R

Em7

7fr
1 3 1 2 1
R

Em7

2fr
1 3 2 2
R

Em7

12fr
2 3 3 3 3
R

E

Minor Seventh Chords with Alterations

Em7♭5

1 3 2 4
R

Em7♭5

2 3 4 1
R

Em7♭5

1 3 1 2
R

Em7♭5

2 3 1 4
R

Minor-Major Seventh [m(maj7), m/M7]

Em(maj7)

2 1
R

Em(maj7)

1 4 2 3 1
R

Em(maj7)

2 3 1 4
R

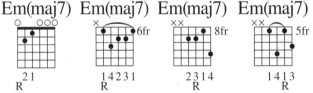

Em(maj7)

1 4 1 3
R

Diminished Seventh (°7)

E°7

2 3 1 4
R

E°7

1 3 2 4
R

E°7

2 1 3 1
R

E°7

2 1 4 1
R

E

Ninth Chords

Dominant Ninth (9)

E9
× ×   6fr
2 1 3 4
R

E9
× ×   11fr
1 3 2 4

E9
×   6fr
2 1 3 3 3

E9
× ×
2 1 4 3
R

Dominant Ninth Chords with Alterations

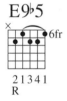
E9♭5
×   6fr
2 1 3 4 1
R

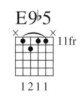
E9♭5
×   ×   11fr
1 2 1 1

E9♭5
×   ○   6fr
1 2 3 4
R

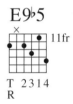
E9♭5
×   11fr
T 2 3 1 4
R

E9♯5
×   6fr
2 1 3 3 4
R

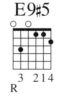
E9♯5
○   ○
3   2 1 4
R

E9♯5
×   11fr
1 2 1 4 3
R

E9♯5
×   ×   6fr
4 1 2 3

E

Major Ninth (maj9, M9, ma9, △9)

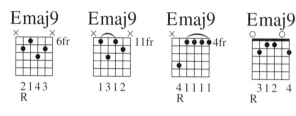

Minor Ninth (m9, min9, -9)

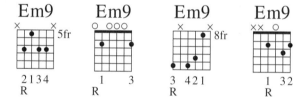

Minor Ninth Chords with Alterations

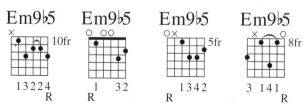

E

Minor-Major Ninth [m(maj9), m/M9]

Em(maj9)
× × 5fr
2 1 4 3
R

Em(maj9)
○ ○○
2 1 3
R

Em(maj9)
× × 10fr
1 4 2 3

Em(maj9)
× × ○
1 4 2
R

Eleventh Chords

Dominant Eleventh (11)

E11
× × 5fr
2 3 4 1
R

E11
× 7fr
1 1 1 1 1
R

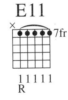

E11
× × 10fr
3 4 2 1
R

E11
× 2fr
1 1 1 2 3
R

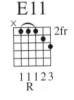

Major Eleventh (maj11, M11, ma11, △11)

Emaj11
○ × 5fr
2 4 3 1
R

Emaj11
× 7fr
1 1 2 3 1
R

Emaj11
× ○ 10fr
2 4 3 1
R

Emaj11
× 2fr
1 1 1 3 3
R

E

Minor Eleventh (m11, min11, -11)

Em11
× ●5fr
2 1 3 4 1
R

Em11
× ●2fr
1 1 1 3 3
R

Em11
× ●7fr
1 1 1 2 1
R

Em11
× ×10fr
2 3 4 1

Thirteenth Chords

Dominant Thirteenth (13)

E13
○ ○   ○
2 1 3
R

E13
×   6fr
2 1 3 3 4
R

E13
× × ○   ○
2 3
R

E13
×   9fr
3 4 2 1 1
R

Dominant 13th Chords with Alterations

E13♯11
×   7fr
1 2 1 3 4
R

E13♯11
○ ○   ×
1 2 3
R

E13♯11
×   5fr
1 3 2 1 4
R

E13♯11
×   10fr
1 2 2 3 3 4
R

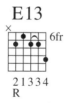
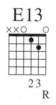
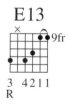

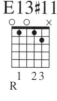

E

E13♭9

9fr

3 4 2 1 1
R

E13♭9

6fr

1 2 1 4

E13♭9

1 3 2

E13♭9

5fr

1 3 3 3
R

E13♯9

6fr

1 2 3 4
R

E13♯9

11fr

1 2 3 4
R

E13♯9

1 2 3

E13♯9

5fr

1 2 3 4
R

Major Thirteenth (maj13, M13, ma13, △13)

Emaj13

3 1 2 4
R

Emaj13

9fr

3 4 2 1 1
R

Emaj13

7fr

1 2 3 4
R

Emaj13

9fr

2 3 1 4
R

E

Major 13th Chords with Alterations

Emaj13#11

1234
R

Emaj13#11

12234
R

Emaj13#11

2 1311
R

Emaj13#11

1243
R

Minor Thirteenth (m13, min13, -13)

Em13

1 3
R

Em13

1 234
R

Em13

13124
R

Em13
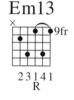
23141
R

Minor 13th Chords with Alterations

Em13♭5

1 32
R

Em13♭5

12134
R

Em13♭5

3421
R

Em13♭5
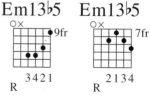
2134
R

E

Sixth Chords

Sixth Chords (6)

E6

×   ×   11fr

2   1 4 3
R

E6

×   5fr

4 2 3 1
R

E6

×   7fr

1 3 3 3 3
R

E6

○   ○

2 3 1 4
R

Six-Nine Chords ($^6_9$)

E^6_9

×   6fr

2 1 1 3 4
R

E^6_9

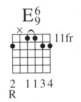

×   11fr

2   1 1 3 4
R

E^6_9

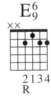

× ×

2 1 3 4
R

E^6_9

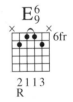

×   ×   6fr

2 1 1 3
R

Minor Sixth Chords (m6)

Em6

×   ×   11fr

2   1 3 4
R

Em6

×   5fr

3 1 2 1
R

Em6

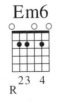

○   ○   ○

2 3   4
R

Em6

× ×   11fr

1 3 3 3
     R

E

Minor Six-Nine Chords (m$^6_9$)

Em^6_9

× × 5fr
3 1 2 4
R

Em^6_9

× × 8fr
3 4 1
R

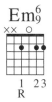

Em^6_9

○
1 2 3
R

Em^6_9

× 11fr
2 1 3 3 4
R

Power Chords ("5" Chords)

E5

○   ○○
1 1 4
R

E5

×   ×× 7fr
1 3 4
R

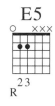

E5

○   ×××
2 3
R

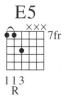

E5

××× 7fr
1 1 3
R

Suspended (sus) and add Chords

Esus2

○   ○○
1 3 4
R

Esus2

× 7fr
1 3 4 1 1
R

Esus2

× × 4fr
4 1 1 2
R

Esus2

× × 11fr
2   1 3 4
R

E

Esus4

××   2fr

1 3 4 4
R

Esus4

×   7fr

1 3 3 4
R

Esus4

○   ○○

2 3 4
R

Esus4

○   ○   4fr

3 4 1 2
R

Esus^2_4

○   ○○

1 4 2
R

Esus^2_4

×   9fr

4   1 3 2
R

Esus^2_4

××   ○

1 2   3
R

Esus^2_4

×   7fr

1 1 4 1 1
R

E7sus4

××   2fr

1 3 2 4
R

E7sus4

○   ○   ○○

2   3
R

E7sus4

×   7fr

1 3 1 4 1
R

E7sus4

○   5fr

2 2 3 1 4
R

E

E9sus4

1 1 1 1 1
R

E9sus4

2 3 1 4
R

E9sus4

1 1 2 1
R

E9sus4

2 3 4
R

E13sus4

1 23
R

E13sus4

1 1 1 1 4
R

E13sus4

2 3
R

E13sus4

3 4 12 1
R

Eadd4

1 1 2 4
R

Eadd4

3 4 1 2 1
R

Eadd4

1 1 3 4 1
R

Eadd4

1 1 3 2 1 1
R

E

Eadd9

2 4 1
R

Eadd9

4fr
3 2 1 4
R

Eadd9

2 1 3
R

Eadd9

7fr
1 2 4 3 1
R

Em(add9)

1 4
R

Em(add9)

4fr
3 2 1 4
R

Em(add9)

2   3
R

Em(add9)

7fr
1 3 4 2 1
R

"No Third" Chords

E7(no 3rd)

4fr
2   1
R

E7(no 3rd)

7fr
1   2
R

E9(no 3rd)

7fr
2 3 4
R

E13(no 3rd)

4fr
2 1 3
R

E

Other Altered Chords

E(♭5)

1234
R

E(♭5)

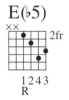

1243
R

E(♭6)

32114
R

E(♭6)

4321
R

Open Voice Triads

E

2 14
R

E

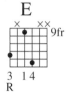

3 14
R

Em

2 14
R

Em

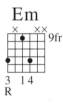

3 14
R

E°

2 14
R

E°

3 14
R

E+

3 14
R

E+

3 14
R

F

Triads

Major

F

1 3 4 2 1 1
R

F

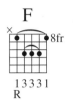

8fr

1 3 3 3 1
R

F

5fr

4 3 1 2 1
R

F

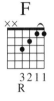

3 2 1 1
R

Minor (m, -)

Fm

1 3 4 1 1 1
R

Fm

8fr

1 3 4 2 1
R

Fm

3fr

1 3 4 2
R

Fm

3 1 1 1
R

Diminished (°, dim)

F°

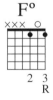

2   3
R

F°

8fr

1 2 4 3
R

F°

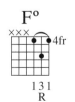

4fr

1 3 1
R

F°

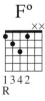

1 3 4 2
R

F

Augmented (+, aug)

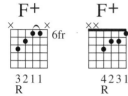

<table>
<tr><td>F+</td><td>F+</td></tr>
</table>

F+   F+   F+   F+

3211
R   4231
R   1432
R   231
R

Seventh Chords
Dominant Seventh (7)

F7   F7   F7   F7

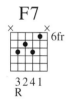
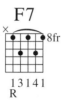

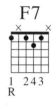

3241
R   13141
R   1324
R   1 243
R

Dominant Seventh Chords with Alterations

F7b5   F7b5   F7b5   F7b5

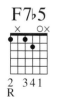

2 341
R   1214
R   2 341
R   2413
R

F

F7♯5

1 234
R

F7♯5

8fr
1 243
R

F7♯5

6fr
4 231
R

F7♯5

6fr
2314
R

F7♭9

7fr
2131
R

F7♭9
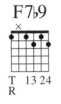
T 1324
R

F7♭9

7fr
2 131

F7♭9

8fr
2314

F7♯9

7fr
2134
R

F7♯9
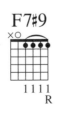
1111
R

F7♯9
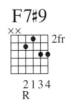
2fr
2134
R

F7♯9
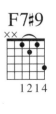
1214

F

F7♭9♭5
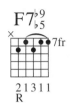
× 7fr
2 1 3 1 1
R

F7♭9♭5

× 12fr
T 2 3 1 4
R

F7♭9♭5

× ○
2 3 4 1
R

F7♭9♭5

× 7fr
1 2 1 3 1
R

F7♯9♯5

× 7fr
2 1 3 1 4
R

F7♯9♯5

×
1 2 4 4 4
R

F7♯9♯5

× 9fr
1 3 2 2 4
R

F7♯9♯5
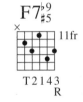
× 11fr
T 2 1 4 3
R

F7♯9♯11

× 7fr
2 1 3 4 1
R

F7♯9♯11
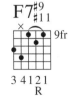
× 9fr
3 4 1 2 1
R

F7♯9♯11

× 7fr
1 2 1 3 4
R

F7♯9♯11

× 3fr
3 1 2 2 2
R

F

$F7^{\sharp 9}_{\sharp 5}$

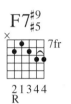

2 1 3 4 4
R

$F7^{\sharp 9}_{\sharp 5}$

13fr

1 2 3 3 4
R

$F7^{\sharp 9}_{\sharp 5}$

12fr

1 2 2 4 3
R

$F7^{\sharp 9}_{\sharp 5}$

12fr

2 1 3 3 4
R

Major Seventh (maj7, M7, ma7, △7)

Fmaj7

8fr

1 3 2 4 1
R

Fmaj7

1   3 4 2
R

Fmaj7

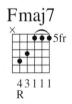

5fr

4 3 1 1 1
R

Fmaj7

3fr

2   1 3 4
R

Major Seventh Chords with Alterations

Fmaj7♭5

3 2

Fmaj7♭5

7fr

2   3 4 1
R

Fmaj7♭5

9fr

1 2 2 4
R

Fmaj7♭5

3fr

1 2 3 3
R

F

Fmaj7#5

1 333
R

Fmaj7#5

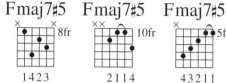

1423
R

Fmaj7#5

8fr

2114
R

Fmaj7#5

43211
R

Fmaj7$^{\#9}_{\#11}$

21341
R

Fmaj7$^{\#9}_{\#11}$

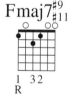

1 32
R

Fmaj7$^{\#9}_{\#11}$

3 1242
R

Fmaj7$^{\#9}_{\#11}$

12fr

14211
R

Minor Seventh (m7, min7, -7)

Fm7

8fr

13121
R

Fm7

131111
R

Fm7

10fr

2314
R

Fm7

6fr

3 143
R

F

Minor Seventh Chords with Alterations

Fm7♭5

Fm7♭5

Fm7♭5

Fm7♭5

1324
R

2 34
R

1312
R

1333
R

Minor-Major Seventh [m(maj7), m/M7]

Fm(maj7)

Fm(maj7)

Fm(maj7)

Fm(maj7)

14231
R

132111
R

2 134
R

2314
R

Diminished Seventh (°7)

F°7

F°7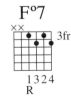

F°7

F°7

2314
R

1324
R

2 131
R

2314
R

F

Ninth Chords

Dominant Ninth (9)

F9

2 1 3 4
R

F9

1 3 2 4

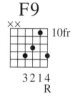

F9

3 2 1 4
R

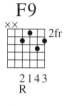

F9

2 1 4 3
R

Dominant Ninth Chords with Alterations

F9♭5

2 1 3 4 1
R

F9♭

1 2 1 1 3
R

F9♭5

1 2 1 3 4
R

F9♭5

T 2 3 1 4
R

F9♯5

2 1 3 3 4
R

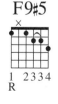

F9♯5

1 2 3 3 4
R

F9♯5

1 2 1 4 3
R

F9♯5

1 3 3 4

F

Major Ninth (maj9, M9, ma9, △9)

Fmaj9

7fr

2 1 4 3
R

Fmaj9

12fr

2 1 4 1 3
R

Fmaj9

3   1
R

Fmaj9
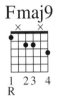

1   2 3   4
R

Minor Ninth (m9, min9, -9)

Fm9

6fr

2 1 3 4
R

Fm9

1 3 1 1 1 4
R

Fm9

11fr

1 3 2 4 4
R

Fm9
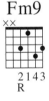

2 1 4 3
R

Minor Ninth Chords with Alterations

Fm9♭5

11fr

1 3 2 2 4
R

Fm9♭5

1 2 1 1 4 3
R

Fm9♭5

6fr

T 2 1 3 4
R

Fm9♭5

9fr

2 1 3 1 4
R

F

Minor-Major Ninth [m(maj9), m/M9]

Fm(maj9)
×   ×
6fr
2 1 4 3
R

Fm(maj9)
1 3 2 1 1 4
R

Fm(maj9)
×× 11fr
3 1 4 2
R

Fm(maj9)
××
2 1 4 3
R

Eleventh Chords

Dominant Eleventh (11)

F11
× ×
6fr
2   3 4 1
R

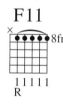
F11
×
8fr
1 1 1 1 1
R

F11
11fr
3   4 2 1
R

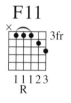
F11
×   ×
3fr
1 1 1 2 3
R

Major Eleventh (maj11, M11, ma11, △11)

Fmaj11
×
6fr
3 2 4 1 1
R

Fmaj11
×
8fr
1 1 2 3 1
R

Fmaj11
×   ○
10fr
3 1 1 2
R

Fmaj11
×
3fr
1 1 1 3 3
R

F

Minor Eleventh (m11, min11, -11)

Fm11

Fm11

Fm11

Fm11

Thirteenth Chords

Dominant Thirteenth (13)

F13

F13

F13

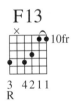

F13

Dominant 13th Chords with Alterations

F13#11

F13#11

F13#11

F13#11

F

F13♭9

3 4211
R

F13♭9

21314
R

F13♭9

1243

F13♭9

1333

F13♯9

1234

F13♯9

12243
R

F13♯9

1234

F13♯9

1224

Major Thirteenth (maj13, M13, ma13, △13)

Fmaj13

1 234
R

Fmaj13

3 4211
R

Fmaj13
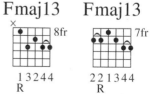
13244
R

Fmaj13
22134 4
R

F

Major 13th Chords with Alterations

Fmaj13#11

1 2 2 3 4
R

Fmaj13#11

8fr

1 2 2 3 4
R

Fmaj13#11

1   3
R

Fmaj13#11

12fr

2 1 1 1 1
R

Minor Thirteenth (m13, min13, -13)

Fm13

1 2 2 4
R

Fm13

1 3 1 1 4 1
R

Fm13

8fr

1 3 1 2 4
R

Fm13

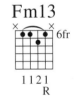

6fr

1 1 2 1
R

Minor 13th Chords with Alterations

Fm13b5

1 2 1 1 4 1
R

Fm13b5

8fr

1 2 1 3 4
R

Fm13b5

6fr

1 1 1 2 1 3
R

Fm13b5

6fr

2 1 3 3 4

F

Sixth Chords

Sixth Chords (6)

F6

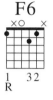

1 3 2
R

F6

1 3 1 4
R
3fr

F6

1 3 3 3 3
R
8fr

F6

3 2 4 1
R

Six-Nine Chords ($^6_9$)

F^6_9

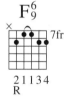

2 1 1 3 4
R
7fr

F^6_9

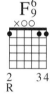

2   3 4
R

F^6_9

2 1 3 4

F^6_9

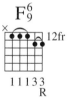

1 1 1 3 3
R
12fr

Minor Sixth Chords (m6)

Fm6

2   3 4
R

Fm6

3 1 2 1 4
R
6fr

Fm6

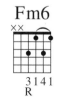

3 1 4 1
R

Fm6

2 3 1 4
R
10fr

F

Minor Six-Nine Chords (m$_9^6$)

Fm$_9^6$

Fm$_9^6$

Fm$_9^6$

Fm$_9^6$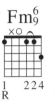

Power Chords ("5" Chords)

F5

F5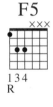

F5

F5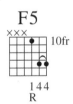

Suspended (sus) and add Chords

Fsus2

Fsus2

Fsus2

Fsus2

F

Fsus4

×× 10fr

1 1 2 4
R

Fsus4

1 2 3 4 1 1
R

Fsus4

×× 3fr

1 3 4 4
R

Fsus4

× × 5fr

3 4 1 2
R

Fsus⁴₂ (Fsus²₄)

○ ×

1 1 4 2
R

Fsus²₄
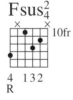
× × 10fr

4 1 3 2
R

Fsus²₄

××

2 3 1 4
R

Fsus²₄

× 8fr

1 1 3 1 1
R

F7sus4

× 8fr

1 3 1 4 1
R

F7sus4

1 3 1 4 1 1
R

F7sus4

×× 3fr

1 3 2 4
R

F7sus4

× × 6fr

2 3 4 1
R

F

F9sus4

1 1 1 1 1
R

F9sus4

11fr

3 2 1 4
R

F9sus4

3fr

1 1 2 1
R

F9sus4

8fr

2 3 3 3

F13sus4

1 1 1 3 4 1
R

F13sus4

8fr

1 1 1 1 4
R

F13sus4

10fr

3 4 2 1
R

F13sus4

8fr

2 3 3 3 4

Fadd4

5fr

3 4 1 2 1
R

Fadd4

8fr

1 1 3 4 1
R

Fadd4

1 1 3 2 1 1
R

Fadd4

13fr

2 2 1 4
R

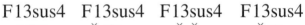

F

Fadd9

3 2 1 4
R

Fadd9
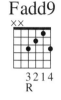

3 2 1 4
R

Fadd9

1 2 4 3 1
R

Fadd9
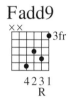

4 2 3 1
R

Fm(add9)

3 2 1 4
R

Fm(add9)

3 1 1 4
R

Fm(add9)

1 3 4 2 1
R

Fm(add9)

3 2 4 1
R

"No Third" Chords

F7(no 3rd)

1 3 2
R

F7(no 3rd)

2 3 1 4
R

F9(no 3rd)

1 3 2 1
R

F13(no 3rd)

T 1 4 2
R

F

Other Altered Chords

F(♭5)

1 2 3 4
R

F(♭5)

1 2 4 3

F(♭6)

3 2 1 1 4

F(♭6)

1 4 3 2 1 1
R

Open Voice Triads

F

3   1 4
R

F
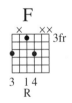
3   1 4
R

Fm

3   1 4
R

Fm

2   1 3
R

F°

3   1 4
R

F°
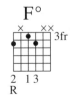
2   1 3
R

F+

3   1 4
R

F+

3   1 4
R

F#/G♭

Triads

Major

Gb
× ●9fr
1 3 3 3 1
R

Gb
1 3 4 2 1 1
R

Gb
× ●6fr
4 3 1 2 1
R

Gb
× × ● ● ●11fr
1 1 1 4
R

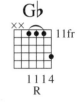

Minor (m, -)

Gbm
× ●9fr
1 3 4 2 1
R

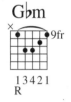

Gbm
1 3 4 1 1 1
R

Gbm
× ×4fr
1 3 4 2
R

Gbm
× ×4fr
2 1 3 4
R

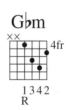

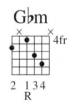

Diminished (°, dim)

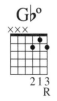

Gb°
× × ×
2 1 3
R

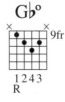

Gb°
× ×9fr
1 2 4 3
R

Gb°
× × ×5fr
1 3 1
R

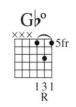

Gb°
× ×
1 3 4 2
R

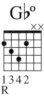

F♯/G♭

Augmented (+, aug)

G♭+

3 2 1 1
R

G♭+

4 2 3 1
R

G♭+

1 4 3 2
R

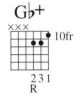

G♭+

2 3 1
R

Seventh Chords
Dominant Seventh (7)

G♭7

3 2 4 1
R

G♭7

1 3 1 4 1
R

G♭7

2 3 1 4
R

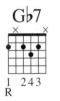

G♭7

1 2 4 3
R

Dominant Seventh Chords with Alterations

G♭7♭5

2 3 4 1
R

G♭7♭5

1 2 1 4
R

G♭7♭5

2 3 4 1
R

G♭7♭5

1 2 3 4
R

F#/G♭

G♭7#5
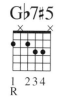
1 234
R

G♭7#5
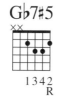
1342
R

G♭7#5

7fr
4 231
R

G♭7#5
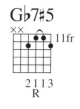
11fr
2113
R

G♭7♭9
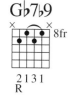
8fr
2131
R

G♭7♭9
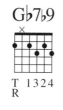
T 1324
R

G♭7♭9

5fr
2 131

G♭7♭9
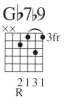
3fr
2131
R

G♭7#9

8fr
2134
R

G♭7#9
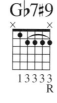
13333
R

G♭7#9

3fr
2134
R

G♭7#9

10fr
3421
R

F#/Gb

$G\flat7^{\flat9}_{\flat5}$

2 1 3 1 1
R

$G\flat7^{\flat9}_{\flat5}$

3 1 4   1
R

$G\flat7^{\flat9}_{\flat5}$
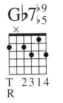
T   2 3 1 4
R

$G\flat7^{\flat9}_{\flat5}$
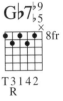
T 3 1 4 2
R

$G\flat7^{\flat9}_{\sharp5}$

2 1 3 1 4
R

$G\flat7^{\flat9}_{\sharp5}$
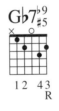
1   2 3 3 3
R

$G\flat7^{\flat9}_{\sharp5}$
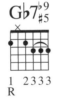
1 2   4 3
R

$G\flat7^{\flat9}_{\sharp5}$
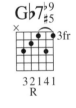
3 2 1 4 1
R

$G\flat7^{\sharp9}_{\sharp11}$
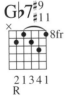
2 1 3 4 1
R

$G\flat7^{\sharp9}_{\sharp11}$
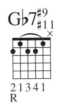
2 1 3 4 1
R

$G\flat7^{\sharp9}_{\sharp11}$

1 2 1 3 4

$G\flat7^{\sharp9}_{\sharp11}$
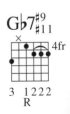
3   1 2 2 2
R

F#/Gb

Gb7#9#5

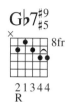

2 1 3 4 4
R

Gb7#9#5

2 1 3 3 4
R

Gb7#9#5

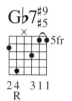

2 4   3 1 1
R

Gb7#9#5

3   1 2 4

Major Seventh (maj7, M7, ma7, △7)

Gbmaj7

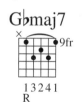

1 3 2 4 1
R

Gbmaj7

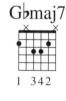

1   3 4 2

Gbmaj7

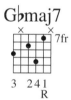

3   2 4 1
R

Gbmaj7

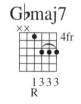

1 3 3 3
R

Major Seventh Chords with Alterations

Gbmaj7b5

4 3 1 1
R

Gbmaj7b5

2   3 4 1
R

Gbmaj7b5

1 2 2 4
R

Gbmaj7b5

4fr

1 2 3 3
R

F#/Gb

Gbmaj7#5

1 .333
R

Gbmaj7#5

9fr

1423
R

Gbmaj7#5

11fr

2114
R

Gbmaj7#5

4fr

43211

Gbmaj7$^{\#9}_{\#11}$

8fr

21341
R

Gbmaj7$^{\#9}_{\#11}$

214311
R

Gbmaj7$^{\#9}_{\#11}$

8fr

12134
R

Gbmaj7$^{\#9}_{\#11}$

13fr

14213
R

Minor Seventh (m7, min7, -7)

Gbm7

9fr

13121
R

Gbm7

10fr

2314
R

Gbm7

2fr

2314
R

Gbm7

2fr

2 333
R

F#/G♭

Minor Seventh Chords with Alterations

G♭m7♭5

G♭m7♭5

G♭m7♭5

G♭m7♭5

Minor-Major Seventh [m(maj7), m/M7]

G♭m(maj7)

G♭m(maj7)

G♭m(maj7)

G♭m(maj7)

Diminished Seventh (°7)

G♭°7

G♭°7

G♭°7

G♭°7

F#/G♭

Ninth Chords

Dominant Ninth (9)

G♭9

8fr

2 1 3 4
R

G♭9

1 3 2 4

G♭9

11fr

3 2 1 4
R

G♭9
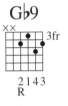
3fr

2 1 4 3
R

Dominant Ninth Chords with Alterations

G♭9♭5

8fr

2 1 3 4 1
R

G♭9♭5

2 1 3 1 1
R

G♭9♭5

8fr

1 2 1 3 4
R

G♭9♭5

2 3 1 4

G♭9♯5

8fr

2 1 3 3 4
R

G♭9♯5

2fr

1 2 3 3 4
R

G♭9♯5

1 2 1 4 3
R

G♭9♯5

7fr

1 2 1 4

F#/G♭

Major Ninth (maj9, M9, ma9, △9)

G♭maj9

G♭maj9

8fr
2143
R

G♭maj9
2141 3
R

G♭maj9

6fr
41111
R

G♭maj9

2fr
14121
R

Minor Ninth (m9, min9, -9)

G♭m9

7fr
21333
R

G♭m9

2fr
131114
R

G♭m9

2 314
R

G♭m9

6fr
3214
R

Minor Ninth Chords with Alterations

G♭m9♭5

2113
R

G♭m9♭5

2fr
121143
R

G♭m9♭5

7fr
T2134
R

G♭m9♭5

5fr
3214
R

F#/Gb

Minor-Major Ninth [m(maj9), m/M9]

Gbm(maj9)　　Gbm(maj9)　　Gbm(maj9)　　Gbm(maj9)

2 1 4 3
R

1 3 2 1 1 4
R

4 1 2 1
R

3 1 4 1

Eleventh Chords

Dominant Eleventh (11)

Gb11　　　Gb11　　　Gb11　　　Gb11

2　3 4 1
R

1 1 1 1 1
R

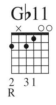
2　3 1
R

3 2
R

Major Eleventh (maj11, M11, ma11, △11)

Gbmaj11　　Gbmaj11　　Gbmaj11　　Gbmaj11

3 4 1 1 1
R

1 1 2 3 1
R

2 1 4　3
R

1 1 1 3 3
R

F#/G♭

Minor Eleventh (m11, min11, -11)

G♭m11

G♭m11

G♭m11

G♭m11

Thirteenth Chords

Dominant Thirteenth (13)

G♭13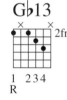

G♭13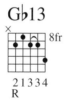

G♭13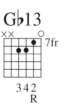

G♭13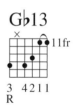

Dominant 13th Chords with Alterations

G♭13#11

G♭13#11

G♭13#11

G♭13#11

F#/Gb

Gb13b9

3 4211
R

Gb13b9

21314
R

Gb13b9

1243

Gb13b9

3112
R

Gb13#9

1234

Gb13#9

12243
R

Gb13#9

1234

Gb13#9

2114
R

Major Thirteenth (maj13, M13, ma13, △13)

Gbmaj13

1   234
R

Gbmaj13

3 4211
R

Gbmaj13

13244
R

Gbmaj13

4231
R

F#/Gb

Major 13th Chords with Alterations

Gbmaj13#11 Gbmaj13#11 Gbmaj13#11 Gbmaj13#11

12224   12244   2 1311   42213
R   R   R   R

Minor Thirteenth (m13, min13, -13)

Gbm13   Gbm13   Gbm13   Gbm13

2 3344   131141   13124   312
R   R   R   R

Minor 13th Chords with Alterations

Gbm13b5   Gbm13b5   Gbm13b5   Gbm13b5

121141   12134   3 142   2 1334
R   R   R   R

F♯/G♭

Sixth Chords

Sixth Chords (6)

Gb6

2 143
R

Gb6
8fr

2314
R

Gb6
9fr

13333
R

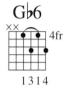
Gb6
4fr

1314

Six-Nine Chords ($^6_9$)

Gb$^6_9$
8fr

21134
R

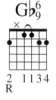
Gb$^6_9$

2 1134
R

Gb$^6_9$
3fr

2134
R

Gb$^6_9$
13fr

11133
R

Minor Sixth Chords (m6)

Gbm6

2 134
R

Gbm6
7fr

3121
R

Gbm6
2fr

3141
R

Gbm6
8fr

2413
R

F♯/G♭

Minor Six-Nine Chords (m⁶₉)

G♭m⁶₉

7fr

3 1 2 4 4
R

G♭m⁶₉

6fr

1 3 2 4
R

G♭m⁶₉

2fr

2 1 3 4
R

G♭m⁶₉

2 1 3 3 4
R

Power Chords ("5" Chords)

G♭5
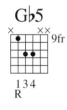

9fr

1 3 4
R

G♭5
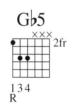

2fr

1 3 4
R

G♭5
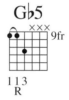

9fr

1 1 3
R

G♭5

4fr

1 1 3 4
R

Suspended (sus) and add Chords

G♭sus2
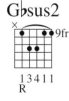

9fr

1 3 4 1 1
R

G♭sus2
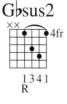

4fr

1 3 4 1
R

G♭sus2
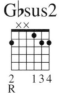

2 1 3 4
R

G♭sus2

6fr

3 1 4
R

F#/G♭

Gbsus4   Gbsus4   Gbsus4   Gbsus4

$Gbsus_4^2$ $Gbsus_4^2$ $Gbsus_4^2$ $Gbsus_4^2$

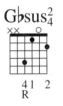

$Gb7sus4$ $Gb7sus4$ $Gb7sus4$ $Gbsus_4^2$

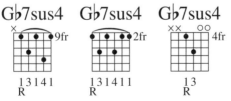

F#/Gb

Gb9sus4

11111
R

Gb9sus4

41
R

Gb9sus4

1121
R

Gb9sus4

21 3
R

Gb13sus4

111341
R

Gb13sus4

11114
R

Gb13sus4

241
R

Gb13sus4

3 4 21
R

Gbadd4

34121
R

Gbadd4

11341
R

Gbadd4

13 4
R

Gbadd4

32 1
R

F#/Gb

Gbadd9

3 2 1 4
R

Gbadd9

3 2 1 4
R

Gbadd9

1 2 4 3 1
R

Gbadd9

1 3 1 4
R

Gbm(add9)

3 2 1 4
R

Gbm(add9)

3 1 1 4
R

Gbm(add9)

1 3 4 2 1
R

Gbm(add9)

2 3 1 4
R

"No Third" Chords

Gb7(no 3rd)

1 3 2
R

Gb7(no 3rd)

1 3 4
R

Gb9(no 3rd)

4 1 2
R

Gb13(no 3rd)

4 1 3
R

F#/G♭

Other Altered Chords

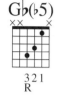

G♭(♭5)

3 2 1
R

G♭(♭5)

4fr

1 2 4 3
R

G♭(♭6)

4fr

4 3 2 1 1
R

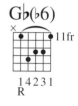

G♭(♭6)

11fr

1 4 2 3 1
R

Open Voice Triads

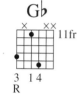

G♭

11fr

3 1 4
R

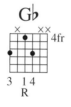

G♭

4fr

3 1 4
R

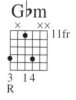

G♭m

11fr

3 1 4
R

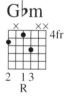

G♭m

4fr

2 1 3
R

G♭°

10fr

3 1 4
R

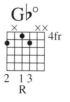

G♭°

4fr

2 1 3
R

G♭+

12fr

3 1 4
R

G♭+

4fr

3 1 4
R

G

Triads

Major

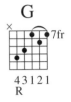

Minor (m, -)

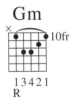

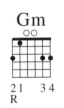

Diminished (°, dim)

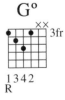

G

Augmented (+, aug)

G+

3 2 1 1
R

G+

4 2 3 1
R

G+

1 4 3 2
R

G+
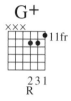
2 3 1
R

Seventh Chords
Dominant Seventh (7)

G7

3 2 4 1
R

G7
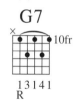
1 3 1 4 1
R

G7

2 3 1 4
R

G7
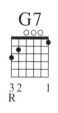
3 2   1
R

Dominant Seventh Chords with Alterations

G7♭5

2   3 4 1
R

G7♭5

1 2 1 4
R

G7♭5

1 2 1 4
R

G7♭5

1 2 2 4
R

G

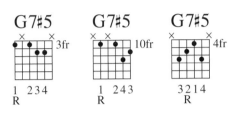

G7♯5

× × 3fr

1 2 3 4
R

G7♯5

× × 10fr

1 2 4 3
R

G7♯5

× 4fr

3 2 1 4
R

G7♯5

× × 3fr

1 3 4 2
R

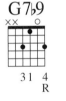

G7♭9

× 9fr

2 1 3 1
R

G7♭9

× 3fr

T 1 3 2 4
R

G7♭9

× × 9fr

2 1 3 1

G7♭9

× × ○

3 1 4
R

G7♯9

× × 9fr

2 1 3 4
R

G7♯9

× × 2fr

2 1 3 3 3
R

G7♯9

× × 4fr

2 1 3 4
R

G7♯9

× 9fr

T 1 2 4 3
R

G

$G7^{\flat 9}_{\flat 5}$

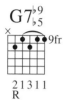

2 1 3 1 1
R

$G7^{\flat 9}_{\flat 5}$

4 2 1   3
R

$G7^{\flat 9}_{\flat 5}$

T   2 3 1 4
R

$G7^{\flat 9}_{\flat 5}$

3 1   4
R

$G7^{\flat 9}_{\sharp 5}$

2 1 3 1 4
R

$G7^{\flat 9}_{\sharp 5}$

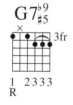

1   2 3 3 3
R

$G7^{\flat 9}_{\sharp 5}$

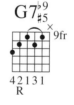

4 2 1 3 1
R

$G7^{\flat 9}_{\sharp 5}$

1 2   3 1

$G7^{\sharp 9}_{\sharp 11}$

2 1 3 4 1
R

$G7^{\sharp 9}_{\sharp 11}$

2 1 3 4 1

$G7^{\sharp 9}_{\sharp 11}$

2 1   4
R

$G7^{\sharp 9}_{\sharp 11}$

2   1 2 2 2
R

G

G7#9#5

9fr

2 1 3 4 4
R

G7#9#5

2fr

2 1 3 3 4
R

G7#9#5

3fr

1 2 3 3 4
R

G7#5

2fr

1 2 2 4 3
R

Major Seventh (maj7, M7, ma7, △7)

Gmaj7

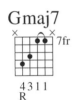

7fr

4 3 1 1
R

Gmaj7

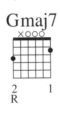

2
R   1

Gmaj7

3fr

1   3 4 2
R

Gmaj7

8fr

2 4 1 3
R

Major Seventh Chords with Alterations

Gmaj7♭5

2   3 4 1
R

Gmaj7♭5

9fr

2   3 4 1
R

Gmaj7♭5

11fr

1 2 2 4
R

Gmaj7♭5

5fr

1 2 3 3
R

G

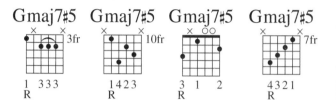

Gmaj7#5   Gmaj7#5   Gmaj7#5   Gmaj7#5

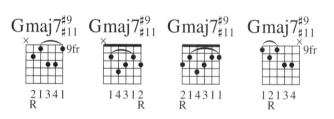

Gmaj7#9#11   Gmaj7#9#11   Gmaj7#9#11   Gmaj7#9#11

Minor Seventh (m7, min7, -7)

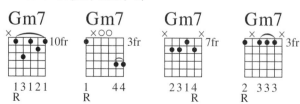

Gm7   Gm7   Gm7   Gm7

G

Minor Seventh Chords with Alterations

Gm7♭5

10fr

1 3 2 4
R

Gm7♭5

2 3 4 1
R

Gm7♭5

8fr

1 3 1 2
R

Gm7♭5

2 3 1 4
R

Minor-Major Seventh [m(maj7), m/M7]

Gm(maj7)

10fr

1 4 2 3 1
R

Gm(maj7)

3fr

1 3 2 1 1 1
R

Gm(maj7)

1   4 3
R

Gm(maj7)

8fr

1 4 1 3
R

Diminished Seventh (°7)

G°7

9fr

2 3 1 4
R

G°7
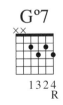

1 3 2 4
R

G°7

2 1 3 1
R

G°7

6fr

2 1 4 1
R

G

Ninth Chords

Dominant Ninth (9)

G9

× 9fr
2 1 3 3 3
R

G9
× 2fr
1 3 2 4

G9

× × ○
3 2   4
R

G9

× × 4fr
2 1 4 3
R

Dominant Ninth Chords with Alterations

G9♭5

× 9fr
2 1 3 4 1
R

G9♭5
2fr
2 1 3 1 1
R

G9♭5

× ○
3 4 2   1
R

G9♭5
× × 9fr
1 2 1 3 4
R

G9♯5
9fr
× 2 1 3 3 4
R

G9♯5

× 3fr
1 2 3 3 4
R

G9♯5

× 2fr
1 2 1 4 3
R

G9♯5

× ○
4 1 3   2
R

G

Major Ninth (maj9, M9, ma9, △9)

Gmaj9

9fr
2 1 4 3
R

Gmaj9

2fr
1 2 4 2 3
R

Gmaj9

3 1 2
R

Gmaj9

3fr
1 3 2   4
R

Minor Ninth (m9, min9, -9)

Gm9

8fr
2 1 3 3 3
R

Gm9

3fr
1 3 1 1 1 4
R

Gm9

5fr
2 4   3 1
R

Gm9

3fr
2 1 4 3
R

Minor Ninth Chords with Alterations

Gm9♭5

1 3 2 2 4
R

Gm9♭5

3fr
1 2 1 1 4 3
R

Gm9♭5

8fr
1 2   4 3
R

Gm9♭5

3fr
T 2 1 4 3
R

G

Minor-Major Ninth [m(maj9), m/M9]

Gm(maj9)   Gm(maj9)   Gm(maj9)   Gm(maj9)

Eleventh Chords

Dominant Eleventh (11)

G11   G11   G11   G11

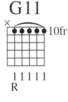
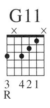

Major Eleventh (maj11, M11, ma11, △11)

Gmaj11   Gmaj11   Gmaj11   Gmaj11

G

Minor Eleventh (m11, min11, -11)

Gm11

× 8fr
2 1 3 4 1
R

Gm11

× 5fr
1 1 1 3 3
R

Gm11
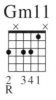
2 3 4 1
R

Gm11

× ○ 8fr
1 2 4 3
R

Thirteenth Chords

Dominant Thirteenth (13)

G13

× × 3fr
1 2 3 4
R

G13

× 9fr
2 1 3 3 4
R

G13

× ○ 9fr
2 3 4 1
R

G13

× ○○
2 3 1
R

Dominant 13th Chords with Alterations

G13♭5

× 10fr
1 2 1 3 4
R

G13♭5

× ○ 6fr
2 4 1 3
R

G13♭5
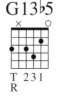
× ○
T 2 3 1
R

G13♭5
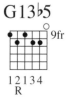
× ○ 9fr
1 2 1 3 4
R

G

G13♭9

3 4 1
R

G13♭9
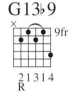

9fr

2 1 3 1 4
R

G13♭9

3fr

1 2 4 3

G13♭9

6fr

3 1
R

G13♯9

9fr

1 2 3 4

G13♯9

2fr

1 2 2 4 3
R

G13♯9

3fr

1 2 3 4

G13♯9

8fr

1 2 4 3
R

Major Thirteenth (maj13, M13, ma13, △13)

Gmaj13

3fr

1 2 3 4
R

Gmaj13
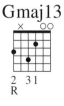

2 3 1
R

Gmaj13

3fr

1 3 2
R

Gmaj13
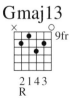

9fr

2 1 4 3
R

G

Major 13th Chords with Alterations

Gmaj13#11   Gmaj13#11   Gmaj13#11   Gmaj13#11

3fr
1 2 2 2 4
R

10fr
1 2 2 4 4
R

2fr
2   1 3 1 1
R

10fr
1 2 3
R

Minor Thirteenth (m13, min13, -13)

Gm13   Gm13   Gm13   Gm13

3fr
2   3 3 4 4
R

3fr
1 3 1 1 4 1
R

10fr
1 3 1 2 4
R

8fr
2 1 3 4
R

Minor 13th Chords with Alterations

Gm13♭5   Gm13♭5   Gm13♭5   Gm13♭5

3fr
1 2 1 1 4 1
R

10fr
1 2 1 3 4
R

2   3 4 1
R

10fr
1 3 2 4
R

G

Sixth Chords

Sixth Chords (6)

G6

2 143
R

G6

○○○○

32
R

G6

10fr

13333
R

G6

3fr

3241
R

Six-Nine Chords ($^6_9$)

G$^6_9$

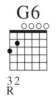

9fr

21134
R

G$^6_9$

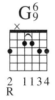

2 1134
R

G$^6_9$

4fr

2134
R

G$^6_9$

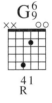

○○

41
R

Minor Sixth Chords (m6)

Gm6

2 134
R

Gm6

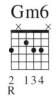

8fr

31214
R

Gm6

3fr

3141
R

Gm6

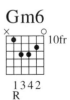

○

10fr

1342
R

G

Minor Six-Nine Chords (m$^6_9$)

Gm$^6_9$

× • • • 8fr

3 1 2 4 4
R

Gm$^6_9$

× • • ○ 7fr

3 2 1 4
R

Gm$^6_9$

× × • • 3fr

2 1 3 4
R

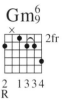

Gm$^6_9$

× • • • • 2fr

2 1 3 3 4
R

Power Chords ("5" Chords)

G5

× ○ ○

2   3 4
R

G5

× × • 10fr

1 3 4
R

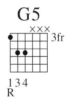

G5

× × × 3fr

1 3 4
R

G5

× × × 10fr

1 1 3
R

Suspended (sus) and add Chords

Gsus2

× × ○

3 1 4
R

Gsus2

× 10fr

1 3 4 1 1
R

Gsus2

× × 5fr

1 3 4 1
R

Gsus2

× ○

2   1 3 4

G

Gsus4
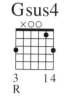

× ○ ○

3   1 4
R

Gsus4

×   × 10fr

1 3 3 4
R

Gsus4
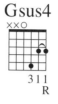

× × ○

3 1 1
      R

Gsus4
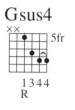

× ×   5fr

1 3 4 4
R

Gsus$_4^2$

×   ×   7fr

3   2 4 1
R

Gsus$_4^2$
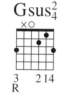

× ○

3   2 1 4
R

Gsus$_4^2$
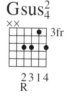

× ×   3fr

2 3 1 4
R

Gsus$_4^2$
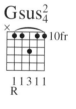

×   10fr

1 1 3 1 1
R

G7sus4

×   10fr

1 3 1 4 1
R

G7sus4
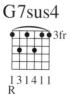

     3fr

1 3 1 4 1 1
R

G7sus4

× ×   5fr

1 3 2 4
R

G7sus4
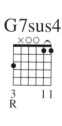

× ○ ○

3   1 1
R

G

G9sus4

10fr

1 1 1 1 1
R

G9sus4

3 2 1 1
R

G9sus4

5fr

1 1 2 1
R

G9sus4

3 4 2 1
R

G13sus4

3fr

1 1 1 3 4 1
R

G13sus4

10fr

1 1 1 1 3
R

G13sus4

10fr

1 3 1 4
R

G13sus4

4 3 2 1
R

Gadd4

7fr

3 4 1 2 1
R

Gadd4

10fr

1 1 3 4 1
R

Gadd4

3 2 1 4

Gadd4

3 4 1
R

G

Gadd9

3 2 4
R

Gadd9

3fr

3214
R

Gadd9

10fr

12431
R

Gadd9

5fr

14 2

Gm(add9)

7fr

3214
R

Gm(add9)

3fr

3114
R

Gm(add9)

10fr

13421
R

Gm(add9)

5fr

3241
R

"No Third" Chords

G7(no 3rd)

3 41
R

G7(no 3rd)
3fr

1 4
R

G9(no 3rd)

2134
R

G13(no 3rd)

2 314
R

G

Other Altered Chords

G(♭5)

10fr
1234
R

G(♭5)

2 3   1
R

G(♭6)

8fr
3 2 1 1 4
R

G(♭6)
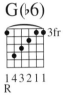
3fr
1 4 3 2 1 1
R

Open Voice Triads

G

3   4
R

G

5fr
3   1 4
R

Gm

3   4
R

Gm

5fr
2   1 3
R

G°

11fr
3   1 4
R

G°

5fr
2   1 3
R

G+

3   1 4
R

G+

5fr
3   1 4
R

G♯/A♭

Triads

Major

A♭
×
11fr
1 3 3 3 1
R

A♭
4fr
1 3 4 2 1 1
R

A♭
×
8fr
4 3 1 2 1
R

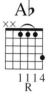

A♭
× ×
1 1 1 4
R

Minor (m, -)

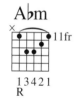

A♭m
×
11fr
1 3 4 2 1
R

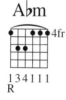

A♭m
4fr
1 3 4 1 1 1
R

A♭m
× ×
6fr
1 3 4 2
R

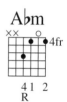

A♭m
× ×   ○
4fr
4 1   2
R

Diminished (°, dim)

A♭°
× × ×
3fr
2 1 3
R

A♭°
×   ×
11fr
1 2 4 3
R

A♭°
× ×   ○
6fr
1 2   3
R

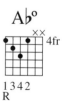

A♭°
× ×   × ×
4fr
1 3 4 2
R

G♯/A♭

Augmented (+, aug)

A♭+
9fr
3 2 1 1
R

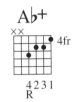

A♭+
4fr
4 2 3 1
R

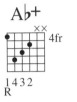

A♭+
4fr
1 4 3 2
R

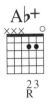

A♭+
2 3
R

Seventh Chords
Dominant Seventh (7)

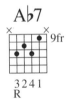

A♭7
9fr
3 2 4 1
R

A♭7
11fr
1 3 1 4
R

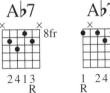

A♭7
8fr
2 4 1 3
R

A♭7
4fr
1 2 4 3
R

Dominant Seventh Chords with Alterations

A♭7♭5
3fr
2 3 4 1
R

A♭7♭5
11fr
1 2 1 4
R

A♭7♭5
9fr
2 3 4 1
R

A♭7♭5
9fr
2 4 1 3
R

G#/A♭

A♭7#5

1 2 3 4
R

A♭7#5

1 2 4 3
R

A♭7#5

1 3 4 2
R

A♭7#5

1 4 2 3
R

A♭7♭9

2 1 3 1
R

A♭7♭9

T 1 3 2 4
R

A♭7♭9

2 1 3 1
R

A♭7♭9

2 3 1 4

A♭7#9

2 1 3 4
R

A♭7#9

2 1 3 3 3
R

A♭7#9

2 1 3 4
R

A♭7#9

1 2 1 4

G♯/A♭

$Ab7^{b9}_{b5}$

10fr

2 1 3 1 1
R

$Ab7^{b9}_{b5}$

5fr

1 2 1 3 1
R

$Ab7^{b9}_{b5}$

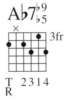

3fr

T 2 3 1 4
R

$Ab7^{b9}_{b5}$

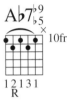

10fr

1 2 1 3 1
R

$Ab7^{b9}_{\#5}$

10fr

2 1 3 1 4
R

$Ab7^{b9}_{\#5}$

4fr

1 2 3 3 3
R

$Ab7^{b9}_{\#5}$

8fr

4 2 1 3 1
R

$Ab7^{b9}_{\#5}$

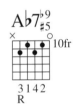

10fr

3 1 4 2
R

$Ab7^{\#9}_{\#11}$

10fr

2 1 3 4 1
R

$Ab7^{\#9}_{\#11}$

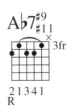

3fr

2 1 3 4 1
R

$Ab7^{\#9}_{\#11}$

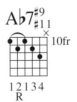

10fr

1 2 1 3 4
R

$Ab7^{\#9}_{\#11}$

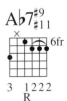

6fr

3 1 2 2 2
R

G♯/A♭

Ab7♯9♯5
×
10fr
2 1 3 4 4
R

Ab7♯9♯5
3fr
2 1 3 3 4
R

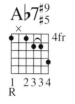

Ab7♯9♯5
×
4fr
1   2 3 3 4
R

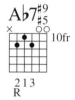

Ab7♯9♯5
× ○○
10fr
2 1 3
R

Major Seventh (maj7, M7, ma7, △7)

Abmaj7
×
11fr
1 3 2 4 1
R

Abmaj7
×   ×
4fr
1   3 4 2
R

Abmaj7
×
9fr
3   2 4 1
R

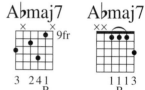

Abmaj7
× ×
1 1 1 3
R

Major Seventh Chords with Alterations

Abmaj7b5
×
3fr
2   4 3 1 1
R

Abmaj7b5
× ×
10fr
2   3 4 1
R

Abmaj7b5
×× ○
1 1 3
R

Abmaj7b5
× ×
6fr
1 2 3 3
R

G♯/A♭

A♭maj7♯5

```
  ×   ×
              4fr
●  ● ● ●


1  3 3 3
R
```

A♭maj7♯5

```
  ×        ×
              11fr
●
   ●     ●
      ●

1 4 2 3
R
```

A♭maj7♯5

```
×  ×
        ┌──┐
●  ● ● ●


2 1 1 4
R
```

A♭maj7♯5

```
×  ×        ○
              5fr
   ●  ●

         ●

2  1 4
R
```

A♭maj7♯9♯11

```
  ×   ┌───┐
              10fr
●  ● ●    ●
   ●  ●


2 1 3 4 1
R
```

A♭maj7♯9♯11

```
              3fr
●  ● ●
   ●  ●  ●
      ●

2 1 4 3 1
R
```

A♭maj7♯9♯11

```
  ×        ○
              10fr
●  ● ●
         ●

         ●
2 1 4  3
R
```

A♭maj7♯9♯11

```
  ┌────┐    ×
              10fr
●  ● ● ●
      ●  ●


1 2 1 3 4
R
```

Minor Seventh (m7, min7, -7)

A♭m7

```
×  ┌─────┐
              11fr
●  ● ●   ●
      ●


1 3 1 2 1
R
```

A♭m7

```
┌──────────┐
●  ● ● ● ● ●      4fr



1 3 1 1 1 1
R
```

A♭m7

```
×  ×  ┌───┐
              9fr
   ●  ● ● ●

      ●

1 3 1 4
R
```

A♭m7

```
  ×        ×
              6fr
●     ●
   ●     ●

2  1 4 3
R
```

G♯/A♭

Minor Seventh Chords with Alterations

A♭m7♭5

A♭m7♭5

A♭m7♭5

A♭m7♭5

Minor-Major Seventh [m(maj7), m/M7]

A♭m(maj7) A♭m(maj7) A♭m(maj7) A♭m(maj7)

Diminished Seventh (°7)

A♭°7

A♭°7

A♭°7

A♭°7

G#/Ab

Ninth Chords

Dominant Ninth (9)

Ab9

10fr
2 1 3 4
R

Ab9

3fr
1 3 2 4

Ab9

3 2 1 4
R

Ab9

5fr
2 1 4 3
R

Dominant Ninth Chords with Alterations

Ab9#11

10fr
2 1 3 4 1
R

Ab9#11

3fr
1 2 1 1 3
R

Ab9#11

5fr
1 2 1 4 3
R

Ab9#11

10fr
1 2 1 3 4
R

Ab9#5

10fr
2 1 3 3 4
R

Ab9#5

4fr
1 2 3 3 4
R

Ab9#5

3fr
2 1 3 1 4
R

Ab9#5

3 4 2 1
R

G♯/A♭

Major Ninth (maj9, M9, ma9, △9)

A♭maj9
×   ×   10fr
2 1 4 3
R

A♭maj9
× 3fr
2 1 4 1 3
R

A♭maj9
× 8fr
4 1 1 1 1
R

A♭maj9
×
4   1 2 1 3
R

Minor Ninth (m9, min9, -9)

A♭m9
×   ×   9fr
2 1 3 4
R

A♭m9
× ×
1 1 1 4

A♭m9
× 2fr
1 3 2 4 4
R

A♭m9
× × 4fr
2 1 4 3
R

Minor Ninth Chords with Alterations

A♭m9♭5
× 2fr
1 3 2 2 4
R

A♭m9♭5
4fr
1 2 1 1 4 3
R

A♭m9♭5
○ ×
8fr
2 3 1 4
R

A♭m9♭5
× 4fr
T 2 1 4 3
R

G#/A♭

Minor-Major Ninth [m(maj9), m/M9]

A♭m(maj9) A♭m(maj9) A♭m(maj9) A♭m(maj9)

Eleventh Chords

Dominant Eleventh (11)

A♭11 A♭11 A♭11 A♭11

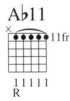

Major Eleventh (maj11, M11, ma11, △11)

A♭maj11 A♭maj11 A♭maj11 A♭maj11

G♯/A♭

Minor Eleventh (m11, min11, -11)

A♭m11

9fr
2 1 3 4 1
R

A♭m11

6fr
1 1 1 3 3
R

A♭m11

2fr
2   3 4 1
R

A♭m11

9fr
3 1 4 1 1
R

Thirteenth Chords

Dominant Thirteenth (13)

A♭13

4fr
1 2 3 4
R

A♭13

10fr
2 1 3 3 4
R

A♭13

4fr
1 2 3 1
R

A♭13

3 4 2 1 1
R

Dominant 13th Chords with Alterations

A♭13♯11

11fr
1 2 1 3 4
R

A♭13♯11

4fr
2 1 3 4 1
R

A♭13♯11

10fr
1 2 1 3 3 4
R

A♭13♯11

6fr
4 1 2 1 3
R

G#/Ab

Ab13b9

3 4211
R

Ab13b9

10fr
21314
R

Ab13b9

4fr
1243

Ab13b9

9fr
1333

Ab13#9

10fr
1234

Ab13#9

3fr
21334
R

Ab13#9

4fr
1234

Ab13#9

9fr
1224

Major Thirteenth (maj13, M13, ma13, △13)

Abmaj13

4fr
1 234
R

Abmaj13

3 4211
R

Abmaj13

11fr
13244
R

Abmaj13

4fr
2341
R

G#/Ab

Major 13th Chords with Alterations

Abmaj13#11   Abmaj13#11   Abmaj13#11   Abmaj13#11

4fr   11fr   3fr   8fr

1 2 2 2 4   1 2 2 4 4   2   1 3 1 1   3 4 2 1 1
R   R   R   R

Minor Thirteenth (m13, min13, -13)

Abm13   Abm13   Abm13   Abm13

4fr   4fr   11fr   9fr

2   3 3 4   1 3 1 1 4 1   1 3 1 2 4   2 1 3 3 4
R   R   R   R

Minor 13th Chords with Alterations

Abm13b5   Abm13b5   Abm13b5   Abm13b5

4fr   11fr   10fr   9fr

1 2 1 1 4 1   1 2 1 3 4   4 2 3 1   T 2 1 3 3 4
R   R   R   R

G#/Ab

Sixth Chords

Sixth Chords (6)

Ab6
2 143
R

Ab6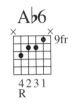
4231
R

Ab6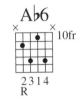
2314
R

Ab6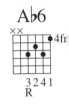
3241
R

Six-Nine Chords ($\frac{6}{9}$)

Ab$\frac{6}{9}$
21134
R

Ab$\frac{6}{9}$
211134
R

Ab$\frac{6}{9}$
2134
R

Ab$\frac{6}{9}$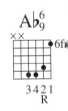
3421
R

Minor Sixth Chords (m6)

Abm6
2 134
R

Abm6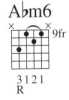
3121
R

Abm6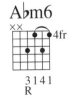
3141
R

Abm6
2431
R

G♯/A♭

Minor Six-Nine Chords (m$_9^6$)

A♭m$_9^6$

× × 9fr
3 1 2 4
R

A♭m$_9^6$

× 3fr
2 1 3 3 4
R

A♭m$_9^6$

× × 4fr
2 1 3 4
R

A♭m$_9^6$

× × 6fr
2 4 3 1
R

Power Chords ("5" Chords)

A♭5

× 11fr
1 3 4
R

A♭5

× × × 4fr
1 3 4
R

A♭5

× × 6fr
1 1 3 4
R

A♭5

× ×
1 1 4 4
R

Suspended (sus) and add Chords

A♭sus2

× 11fr
1 3 4 1 1
R

A♭sus2

× × 6fr
1 3 4 1
R

A♭sus2
× ×
3   1 2 4

A♭sus2

× × 8fr
1 1 2 4

G#/A♭

Absus4

1 3 3 4
R
11fr

Absus4

3 4 1 1
R
4fr

Absus4

1 1 3 4 1 1
R
4fr

Absus4

3 4 1 2
R
8fr

A♭sus$^2_4$

3 2 4 1
R
8fr

A♭sus$^2_4$

4 1 3 2
R

A♭sus$^2_4$

2 3 1 4
R
4fr

A♭sus$^2_4$

1 1 4 1 1
R
6fr

A♭7sus4

1 3 1 4 1
R
11fr

A♭7sus4

1 3 1 4 1 1
R
4fr

A♭sus$^2_4$

2 3 4 1
R
9fr

A♭7sus4

2 1 1 3
R

G♯/A♭

A♭9sus4

11fr
× ●●●●●
1 1 1 1 1
R

A♭9sus4

3fr
T 2 3 1 4
R

A♭9sus4

6fr
× × ●●●●
1 1 2 1
R

A♭9sus4

8fr
× ●●●● ×
2 1 4 3
R

A♭13sus4

4fr
1 1 1 3 4 1
R

A♭13sus4

11fr
× ●●●●
1 1 1 1 3
R

A♭13sus4
4fr
× ×
1 3 4 2
R

A♭13sus4
9fr
× ×
1 4 3 2
R

A♭add4

8fr
×
3 4 1 2 1
R

A♭add4
11fr
×
1 1 3 4 1
R

A♭add4

6fr
× ×
1 1 4 3

A♭add4

2fr
× ×
4 3 1
R

G#/A♭

A♭add9

× × 8fr
3 2 1 4
R

A♭add9

× × 4fr
3 2 1 4
R

A♭add9

× 11fr
1 2 4 3 1
R

A♭add9

4fr
1 3 4 2 1 1
R

A♭m(add9)

× 8fr
3 2 1 4
R

A♭m(add9)
× × 4fr
3 1 1 4
R

A♭m(add9)

× 11fr
1 3 4 2 1
R

A♭m(add9)

4fr
1 3 4 1 1 1
R

"No Third" Chords

A♭7(no 3rd)

× × × ×
2   1 1
R

A♭7(no 3rd)

× ×   ×
3 1 4
R

A♭7(no 3rd)

× ×   × 3fr
3 1 4
R

A♭7(no 3rd)

×   × 7fr
4 2 3 1
R

G♯/A♭

Other Altered Chords

Ab(b5)
11fr
1 2 3 4
R

Ab(b5)
3fr
4 3 1 2
R

Ab(b6)
9fr
3 2 1 1 4
R

Ab(b6)
4fr
3 2 1
R

Open Voice Triads

Ab
3 1 4
R

Ab
6fr
3 1 4
R

Abm
6fr
3 1 4
R

Abm
6 fr
2 1 3
R

Ab°
11fr
3 4
R

Ab°
6fr
2 1 3
R

Ab+
3 1 4
R

Ab+
6fr
3 1 4
R

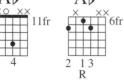

A

Triads

Major

A
× ○　　　 ○
1 2 3
R

A
5fr
1 3 4 2 1 1
R

A
×
9fr
4 3 1 2 1
R

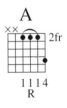
A
× ×
2fr
1 1 1 4
R

Minor (m, -)

Am
× ○　　　 ○
2 3 1
R

Am
5fr
1 3 4 1 1 1
R

Am
× ×
7fr
1 3 4 2
R

Am
× ×　　　 ×
9fr
2 1 3
R

Diminished (°, dim)

A°
× × ×
4fr
2 1 3
R

A°
× ○　　　 ×
1 3 2
R

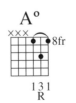
A°
× × ×
8fr
1 3 1
R

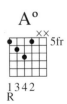
A°
× ×
5fr
1 3 4 2
R

A

Augmented (+, aug)

A+
2fr
3 2 1 1
R

A+
5fr
4 2 3 1
R

A+
5fr
1 4 3 2
R

A+
9fr
2 3 1
R

Seventh Chords
Dominant Seventh (7)

A7
2 3
R

A7
5fr
1 3 1 2 1 1
R

A7
7fr
3 1 4 2
R

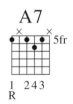

A7
5fr
1 2 4 3
R

Dominant Seventh Chords with Alterations

A7♭5
4fr
2 3 4 1
R

A7♭5
1 3
R

A7♭5
10fr
2 3 4 1
R

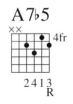

A7♭5
4fr
2 4 1 3
R

A

A7#5

1 234
R

A7#5

3 21
R

A7#5

4 231
R

A7#5

1342
R

A7♭9

2131
R

A7♭9

T 1324
R

A7♭9

14 23
R

A7♭9

2131
R

A7#9

2134
R

A7#9

1333

A7#9

2134
R

A7#9

1214
R

A

$A7^{\flat 9}_{\flat 5}$

```
2 1 3 1 1
R
```

$A7^{\flat 9}_{\flat 5}$

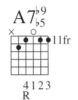

```
4 1 2 3
R
```

$A7^{\flat 9}_{\flat 5}$

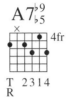

```
T  2 3 1 4
R
```

$A7^{\flat 9}_{\flat 5}$

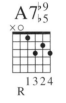

```
1 3 2 4
R
```

$A7^{\flat 9}_{\sharp 5}$

```
2 1 3 1 4
R
```

$A7^{\flat 9}_{\sharp 5}$

```
1  2 3 3 3
R
```

$A7^{\flat 9}_{\sharp 5}$

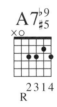

```
2 3 1 4
R
```

$A7^{\flat 9}_{\sharp 5}$

```
1 2 1 3 1
R
```

$A7^{\sharp 9}_{\sharp 11}$

```
2 1 3 4 1
R
```

$A7^{\sharp 9}_{\sharp 11}$

```
2 1 3 4 1
R
```

$A7^{\sharp 9}_{\sharp 11}$

```
1 2 1 3 4
R
```

$A7^{\sharp 9}_{\sharp 11}$

```
3  1 2 2 2
```

A

$A7^{\sharp 9}_{\sharp 5}$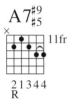

$A7^{\sharp 9}_{\sharp 5}$

$A7^{\sharp 9}_{\sharp 5}$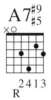

$A7^{\sharp 9}_{\sharp 5}$

Major Seventh (maj7, M7, ma7, △7)

Amaj7

Amaj7

Amaj7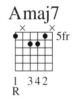

Amaj7

Major Seventh Chords with Alterations

Amaj7♭5

Amaj7♭5

Amaj7♭5

Amaj7♭5

A

Amaj7#5

5fr

1 3 3 3
R

Amaj7#5

3 1 2 1
R

Amaj7#5

6fr

3 2 1 4
R

Amaj7#5

2fr

2 3 1 4
R

Amaj7$^{\sharp 9}_{\sharp 11}$

11fr

2 1 3 4 1
R

Amaj7$^{\sharp 9}_{\sharp 11}$

4fr

2 1 4 3 1
R

Amaj7$^{\sharp 9}_{\sharp 11}$

11fr

1 2 1 3 4
R

Amaj7$^{\sharp 9}_{\sharp 11}$

4fr

1 4 2 1 1
R

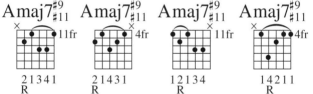

Minor Seventh (m7, min7, -7)

Am7

2   1
R

Am7

5fr

1 3 1 1 1 1
R

Am7

2 3 1 4
R

Am7

5fr

1 1 1 1
R

A

Minor Seventh Chords with Alterations

Am7♭5

2 3
R

Am7♭5

2 341
R

Am7♭5

2314
R

Am7♭5

1214
R

Minor-Major Seventh [m(maj7), m/M7]

Am(maj7)

312
R

Am(maj7)

132111
R

Am(maj7)

2214
R

Am(maj7)

2111
R

Diminished Seventh (°7)

A°7

2314
R

A°7

1324
R

A°7

2 131
R

A°7
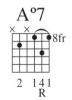

2 141
R

Ninth Chords

Dominant Ninth (9)

A9
×○ ○
4 3 1
R

A9
× × 11fr
2 1 3 4
R

A9
×× ○○ 7fr
1   4
R

A9
×× 6fr
2 1 4 3
R

Dominant Ninth Chords with Alterations

  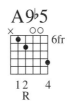

A9♭5
× 11fr
2 1 3 4 1
R

A9♭5
× 4fr
2 1 3 1 1
R

A9♭5
× ○○ 6fr
1 2   4
R

A9♭5
×○ 4fr
2 3 1 4
R

A9♯5
× 11fr
2 1 3 3 4
R

A9♯5
× 5fr
1   2 3 3 4
R

A9♯5
× ○○ 7fr
2 1   4
R

A9♯5
× 4fr
1 2 1 4 3
R

A

Major Ninth (maj9, M9, ma9, △9)

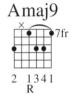

Minor Ninth (m9, min9, -9)

Minor Ninth Chords with Alterations

A

Minor-Major Ninth [m(maj9), m/M9]

Eleventh Chords

Dominant Eleventh (11)

 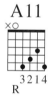 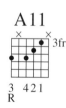 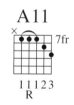

Major Eleventh (maj11, M11, ma11, △11)

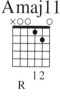 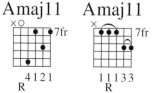

A

Minor Eleventh (m11, min11, -11)

Am11

2 1 3 4 1
R

Am11

1 1 1 3 3
R

Am11

1
R

Am11

2 3 4 1
R

Thirteenth Chords

Dominant Thirteenth (13)

A13

1 2 3 4
R

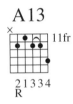

A13

2 1 3 3 4
R

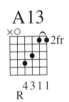

A13

4 3 1 1
R

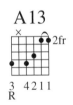

A13

3 4 2 1 1
R

Dominant 13th Chords with Alterations

A13#11

1 2 3
R

A13#11

1 2 1 3 4
R

A13#11

3 4 2 1
R

A13#11

2 3 1 4
R

A

A13♭9

3 4 2 1 1
R

A13♭9

2 1 3 1 4
R

A13♭9

1 2 4 3
R

A13♭9

2 1 3
R

A13#9

1 2 3 4

A13#9

1 2 3 4

A13#9

1 2 3 4
R

A13#9

4 1 2
R

Major Thirteenth (maj13, M13, ma13, △13)

Amaj13

1 2 3 4
R

Amaj13

3 4 2 1 1
R

Amaj13

1 2 3 4
R

Amaj13

4 2 3 1
R

A

Major 13th Chords with Alterations

Amaj13♭5

1 2 2 2 4
R

Amaj13♭5

1 2 3 4
R

Amaj13♭5

2 1 3 1 1
R

Amaj13♭5

2 3 1 4
R

Minor Thirteenth (m13, min13, -13)

Am13

2 3 3 4
R

Am13

1 3 1 1 4 1
R

Am13

2 1 3
R

Am13

4 1
R

Minor 13th Chords with Alterations

Am13♭5

1 2 1 1 4 1
R

Am13♭5

1 2 3
R

Am13♭5

T 2 1 3 3 4
R

Am13♭5

3 4 2 1
R

A

Sixth Chords

Sixth Chords (6)

A6
×   ×   4fr

2 143
R

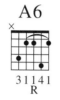

A6
×

31141
R

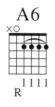

A6
×○

1111
R

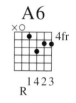

A6
×○   4fr

1423
R

Six-Nine Chords ($^6_9$)

A^6_9
×   11fr

2113
R

A^6_9
×   4fr

11134
R

A^6_9
××   6fr

2134
R

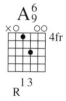

A^6_9
×○   ○○   4fr

13
R

Minor Sixth Chords (m6)

Am6
×   ×   4fr

2 134
R

Am6
×   ×   10fr

3121
R

Am6
×○

2314
R

Am6
×○

1341
R

A

Minor Six-Nine Chords (m⁶₉)

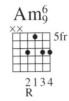
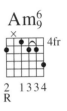

Am^6_9 Am^6_9 Am^6_9 Am^6_9

Power Chords ("5" Chords)

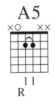
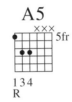

A5   A5   A5   A5

Suspended (sus) and add Chords

Asus2   Asus2   Asus2   Asus2

A

Asus4

1 2 4
R

Asus4

5fr

3 4 1 1
R

Asus4

7fr

1 3 4 4
R

Asus4

1 4 4
R

Asus$^2_4$

9fr

3 2 4 1
R

Asus$^2_4$

2fr

4 1 3 2
R

Asus$^2_4$

7fr

2 3
R

Asus$^2_4$

2
R

A7sus4

1 3
R

A7sus4

5fr

1 3 1 4 1 1
R

A7sus4

7fr

1 3 2 4
R

A7sus4

1 2 4
R

A

A9sus4

R

A9sus4

1 3
R

A9sus4

1 1 2 1
R

A9sus4

4 2 3 1
R

A13sus4

1 1 1 3 4 1
R

A13sus4

2
R

A13sus4

3 1 4
R

A13sus4

4 3 2 1
R

Aadd4

4 3 1
R

Aadd4

4 1 3
R

Aadd4

2 3
R

Aadd4

1 1 3 2 1 1
R

A

Aadd9

142
R

Aadd9

5fr
3214
R

Aadd9

6fr
32
R

Aadd9

7fr
13 4
R

Am(add9)

241
R

Am(add9)

5fr
3114
R

Am(add9)

5fr
31
R

Am(add9)

7fr
13 2
R

No Third" Chords

A7(no 3rd)

1 44
R

A7(no 3rd)

5fr
2   3
R

A9(no 3rd)

5fr
2   3
R

A13(no 3rd)

2   3
R

A

Other Altered Chords

A(♭5)

1 2 3
R

A(♭5)

7fr

1 2 4 3
R

A(♭6)

10fr

3 2 1 1 4
R

A(♭6)

6fr

3 1 2
R

Open Voice Triads

A

2 3
R

A

4fr

1 4 2
R

Am

2 1
R

Am

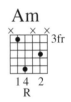

3fr

1 4 2
R

A°

2 3
R

A°

3fr

1 4 2
R

A+

3 2
R

A+

4fr

1 4 3
R

A#/Bb

Triads

Major

Bb

Bb   6fr

Bb   10fr

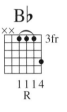

Bb   3fr

1 3 3 3 1
R

1 3 4 2 1 1
R

4 3 1 2 1
R

1 1 1 4
R

Minor (m, -)

Bbm

Bbm   6fr

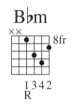

Bbm   8fr

Bbm

1 3 4 2 1
R

1 3 4 1 1 1
R

1 3 4 2
R

3 2 1
R

Diminished (°, dim)

Bb°   5fr

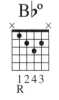

Bb°

Bb°   9fr

Bb°   6fr

2 1 3
R

1 2 4 3
R

1 3 1
R

1 3 4 2
R

A#/B♭

Augmented (+, aug)

B♭+
×   ×
3fr
3 2 1 1
R

B♭+
× ×
6fr
4 2 3 1
R

B♭+
× ×
10fr
1 4 3 2
R

B♭+
× × ×
6fr
2 3 1
R

Seventh Chords
Dominant Seventh (7)

B♭7
6fr
1 3 1 2 1 1
R

B♭7
×
1 3 1 4 1
R

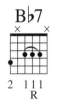

B♭7
×   ×
11fr
3   2 4 1
R

B♭7
×   ×
2   1 1 1
R

Dominant Seventh Chords with Alterations

B♭7♭5
×   ×
5fr
2   3 4 1
R

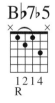

B♭7♭5
×   ×
1 2 1 4
R

B♭7♭5
×   ×
11fr
2   3 4 1
R

B♭7♭5
×   ×
4   1 2 3
R

A#/B♭

B♭7#5

6fr

1 234
R

B♭7#5

1 243
R

B♭7#5

11fr

4 231
R

B♭7#5

2 311
R

B♭7♭9

2 3 4
R

B♭7♭9

6fr

T 1324
R

B♭7♭9

7fr

2131
R

B♭7♭9

2314

B♭7#9

1 243
R

B♭7#9

5fr

13333
R

B♭7#9

7fr

2134
R

B♭7#9

5fr

21333
R

A#/Bb

$Bb7^{b9}_{b5}$

2　3
R

$Bb7^{b9}_{b5}$

4fr

3 T 4 1 2
R

$Bb7^{b9}_{b5}$

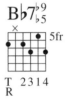

5fr

T　2 3 1 4
R

$Bb7^{b9}_{b5}$

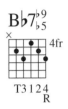

4fr

T 3 1 2 4
　　　　R

$Bb7^{b9}_{#5}$

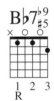

1　2　3
R

$Bb7^{b9}_{#5}$

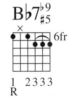

6fr

1　2 3 3 3
R

$Bb7^{b9}_{#5}$

12fr

4 2 1 3 1
R

$Bb7^{b9}_{#5}$

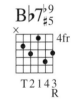

4fr

T 2 1 4 3
　　　　R

$Bb7^{#9}_{#11}$

1　2 3
R

$Bb7^{#9}_{#11}$

5fr

2 1 3 4 1
R

$Bb7^{#9}_{#11}$

12fr

1 2 1 3 4
R

$Bb7^{#9}_{#11}$

8fr

3　1 2 2 2
　　R

A♯/B♭

$Bb7^{#9}_{#5}$

1 234
R

$Bb7^{#9}_{#5}$

5fr

21334
R

$Bb7^{#9}_{#5}$

5fr

12243
R

$Bb7^{#9}_{#5}$

6fr

1 2334
R

Major Seventh (maj7, M7, ma7, △7)

Bbmaj7

13241
R

Bbmaj7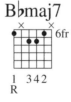

6fr

1 342
R

Bbmaj7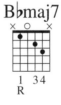

1 34
R

Bbmaj7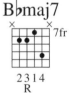

7fr

2314
R

Major Seventh Chords with Alterations

Bbmaj7b5

5fr

4311
R

Bbmaj7b5

1 24
R

Bbmaj7b5

2fr

1224
R

Bbmaj7b5

7fr

1214
R

A#/Bb

Bbmaj7#5

1 333
R

Bbmaj7#5

1423
R

Bbmaj7#5

2114
R

Bbmaj7#5

3214
R

Bbmaj7#9#11

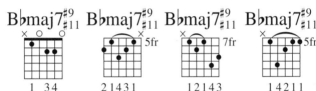

1 34
R

Bbmaj7#9#11

2 1431
R

Bbmaj7#9#11

12143
R

Bbmaj7#9#11

14211
R

Minor Seventh (m7, min7, -7)

Bbm7

13121
R

Bbm7

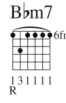

131111
R

Bbm7

1322
R

Bbm7

3 141
R

A♯/B♭

Minor Seventh Chords with Alterations

B♭m7♭5

1 3 2 4
R

B♭m7♭5

5fr

2 3 4 1
R

B♭m7♭5

11fr

1 3 1 2
R

B♭m7♭5

5fr

2 3 1 4
R

Minor-Major Seventh [m(maj7), m/M7]

B♭m(maj7)

1 4 2 3 1
R

B♭m(maj7)

6fr

1 3 2 1 1 1
R

B♭m(maj7)

6fr

1   4 2 3
R

B♭m(maj7)

11fr

1 4 1 3
R

Diminished Seventh (°7)

B♭°7

2 3   4
R

B♭°7

8fr

1 3 2 4
R

B♭°7

5fr

2   1 3 1
R

B♭°7

3fr

2   1 4 1
R

A♯/B♭

Ninth Chords

Dominant Ninth (9)

B♭9

2 333
R

B♭9

5fr

1324

B♭9

3fr

3214
R

B♭9

7fr

2143
R

Dominant Ninth Chords with Alterations

B♭9♭5

2 34
R

B♭9♭5

5fr

12113
R

B♭9♭5

7fr

12143
R

B♭9♭5

5fr

2314

B♭9♯5

1 234
R

B♭9♯5

6fr

1 2334
R

B♭9♯5

5fr

21314
R

B♭9♯5

5fr

12143
R

A♯/B♭

Major Ninth (maj9, M9, ma9, △9)

B♭maj9

× ○

1 4 2 3
R

B♭maj9

5fr

2 1 4 1 3
R

B♭maj9

×
10fr

4 1 1 1 1
R

B♭maj9

×
7fr

2 2 1 4 3

Minor Ninth (m9, min9, -9)

B♭m9

× ×
11fr

2 1 3 4
R

B♭m9

6fr

1 3 1 1 1 4
R

B♭m9

×
4fr

1 3 2 4 4
R

B♭m9

×
6fr

2 2 1 4 3
R

Minor Ninth Chords with Alterations

B♭m9♭5

×
4fr

1 3 2 2 4
R

B♭m9♭5

6fr

1 2 1 1 4 3
R

B♭m9♭5

× ○
11fr

2 1 3 4
R

B♭m9♭5

×
11fr

T 2 1 3 4
R

A#/B♭

Minor-Major Ninth [m(maj9), m/M9]

B♭m(maj9)	B♭m(maj9)	B♭m(maj9)	B♭m(maj9)

Eleventh Chords

Dominant Eleventh (11)

B♭11	B♭11	B♭11	B♭11
	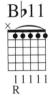		

Major Eleventh (maj11, M11, ma11, △11)

B♭maj11	B♭maj11	B♭maj11	B♭maj11

A#/B♭

Minor Eleventh (m11, min11, -11)

B♭m11

21341
R

B♭m11

11133
R

B♭m11

2 341
R

B♭m11

4211
R

Thirteenth Chords

Dominant Thirteenth (13)

B♭13

1 234
R

B♭13

1 224
R

B♭13

213 4
R

B♭13

3 4211
R

Dominant 13th Chords with Alterations

B♭13#11

12134
R

B♭13#11

12134
R

B♭13#11

341211
R

B♭13#11

T21334
R

A♯/B♭

B♭13♭9

3 4211
R

B♭13♭9

1 2 4
R

B♭13♭9

T 1243
R

B♭13♭9

1333

B♭13#9

1 234
R

B♭13#9

21334
R

B♭13#9

1234

B♭13#9

1224

Major Thirteenth (maj13, M13, ma13, △13)

B♭maj13

1 234
R

B♭maj13

3 4211
R

B♭maj13

12344
R

B♭maj13

1423
R

A#/Bb

Major 13th Chords with Alterations

Bbmaj13#11 Bbmaj13#11 Bbmaj13#11 Bbmaj13#11

6fr
1 2 2 2 4
R

1 2 2 3 4
R

5fr
2 1 3 1 1
R

10fr
4 2 3 1
R

Minor Thirteenth (m13, min13, -13)

Bbm13   Bbm13   Bbm13   Bbm13

6fr
2   3 3 4
R

6fr
1 3 1 1 4 1
R

1 3 1 2 4
R

9fr
4 2 3 1
R

Minor 13th Chords with Alterations

Bbm13b5   Bbm13b5   Bbm13b5   Bbm13b5

6fr
1 2 1 1 4 1
R

1 2 1 3 4
R

11fr
T 2 1 3 3 4
R

11fr
T 1 1 2 1 3
R

A#/Bb

Sixth Chords

Sixth Chords (6)

Bb6
5fr
2 143
R

Bb6
3fr
321 4
R

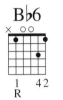

Bb6
1 42
R

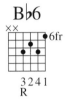

Bb6
6fr
3241
R

Six-Nine Chords (⁶₉)

Bb⁶₉
1 23
R

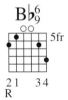

Bb⁶₉
5fr
21 34
R

Bb⁶₉
7fr
2134
R

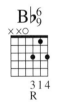

Bb⁶₉
314
R

Minor Sixth Chords (m6)

Bbm6
5fr
2 134
R

Bbm6
11fr
3121
R

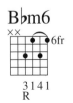

Bbm6
6fr
3141
R

Bbm6
8fr
1312
R

A#/B♭

Minor Six-Nine Chords (m$_9^6$)

B♭m$_9^6$

11fr
3 1 2 4 4
R

B♭m$_9^6$

1 3   2
R

B♭m$_9^6$

6fr
2 1 3 4
R

B♭m$_9^6$

5fr
2   1 3 3 4
R

Power Chords ("5" Chords)

B♭5

1 3 4
R

B♭5
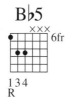
6fr
1 3 4
R

B♭5
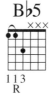
1 1 3
R

B♭5

3fr
1 4 4
R

Suspended (sus) and add Chords

B♭sus2
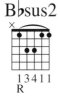
1 3 4 1 1
R

B♭sus2

8fr
1 3 4 1
·R

B♭sus2

5fr
2   1 3 4
R

B♭sus2

10fr
4 1 1 2
R

A♯/B♭

B♭sus4

1 3 3 4
R

B♭sus4

6fr
1 2 3 4 1 1
R

B♭sus4

8fr
1 3 4 4
R

B♭sus4

10fr
3 4 1 2
R

B♭sus$_4^2$

10fr
3 1 4 2
R

B♭sus$_4^2$

3fr
4 1 3 2
R

B♭sus$_4^2$

6fr
2 3 1 4
R

B♭sus$_4^2$

1 1 4 1 1
R

B♭7sus4

1 3 1 4 1
R

B♭7sus4

6fr
1 3 1 4 1 1
R

B♭7sus4

8fr
1 3 2 4
R

B♭7sus4
8fr
4 1 3 2
R

A#/B♭

B♭9sus4

×
1 1 1 1 1
R

B♭9sus4

× ×
5fr
2 3 1 4

B♭9sus4

× ×
8fr
1 1 2 1
R

B♭9sus4

× ×
4fr
3 4 2 1
R

B♭13sus4

6fr
1 1 1 3 4 1
R

B♭13sus4

×
1 1 1 1 4
R

B♭13sus4

× ×
6fr
1 3 4 1
R

B♭13sus4

× ×
3fr
3 4 2 1
R

B♭add4

×
10fr
3 4 1 2 1
R

B♭add4

×
1 1 3 4 1
R

B♭add4

× o ×
1   3 4
R

B♭add4

× ×
4fr
2 4 3 1
R

A♯/B♭

B♭add9

3 2 1 4
R

B♭add9

3 2 1 4
R

B♭add9

3 1 1
R

B♭add9

4 1 1 2 1
R

B♭m(add9)

3 2 1 4
R

B♭m(add9)

3 1 1 4
R

B♭m(add9)

2 1 3 4 4
R

B♭m(add9)

4 2 1 3
R

"No Third" Chords

B♭7(no 3rd)

3 1 4
R

B♭7(no 3rd)

2 4 3 1
R

B♭9(no 3rd)

1 3 1 1 1
R

B♭13(no 3rd)

1 3 1 1 4
R

A♯/B♭

Other Altered Chords

B♭(♭5)

1 2 3 4
R

B♭(♭5)

1　3 4
R

B♭(♭6)

11fr

3 2 1 1 4
R

B♭(♭6)
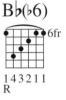
6fr

1 4 3 2 1 1
R

Open Voice Triads

B♭

5fr

1 4　2
R

B♭

8fr

1 4　3
R

B♭m

4fr

1 4　2
R

B♭m

8fr

1 3　4
R

B♭°

4fr

1 4　2
R

B♭°

7fr

1 3　4
R

B♭+

5fr

1 4　3
R

B♭+

9fr

1 4　3
R

B

Triads

Major

B
7fr

1 3 4 2 1 1
R

B

1 3 3 3 1
R

B
11fr

4 3 1 2 1
R

B
4fr

1 1 1 4
R

Minor (m, -)

Bm
7fr

1 3 4 1 1 1
R

Bm

1 3 4 2 1
R

Bm
9fr

1 3 4 2
R

Bm
7fr

1 1 1
R

Diminished (°, dim)

B°
6fr

2 1 3
R

B°

1 2 4 3
R

B°
10fr

1 3 1
R

B°
7fr

1 3 4 2
R

B

Augmented (+, aug)

B+

x O O

2 1 4
R

B+

xx 7fr

4 2 3 1
R

B+

xx 7fr

1 4 3 2
R

B+

xxx 3fr

2 3 1
R

Seventh Chords
Dominant Seventh (7)

B7

x O

2 1 3 4
R

B7

x 2fr

1 3 1 4 1
R

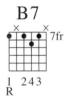

B7

x 4fr

2 1 1 1
R

B7

x x 7fr

1 2 4 3
R

Dominant Seventh Chords with Alterations

B7♭5

x x 6fr

2 3 4 1
R

B7♭5

x x

1 2 1 4
R

B7♭5

x O

3 1 4 2
R

B7♭5

xx 3fr

1 2 3 4
R

B

B7#5

1 234
R

B7#5

1 243
R

B7#5

213 4
R

B7#5

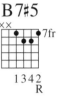

1342
R

B7♭9

2131
R

B7♭9

T 1324
R

B7♭9

1324
R

B7♭9

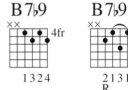

2131
R

B7#9

2134
R

B7#9

21333
R

B7#9

2134
R

B7#9

T 1214
R

B

$B7^{\flat 9}_{\flat 5}$
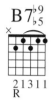
2 1 3 1 1
R

$B7^{\flat 9}_{\flat 5}$

3 T 4 1 2
R

$B7^{\flat 9}_{\flat 5}$
5fr

$B7^{\flat 9}_{\flat 5}$

T   2 3 1 4
R

6fr

$B7^{\flat 9}_{\flat 5}$

T 3 1 2 4
R

5fr

$B7^{\flat 9}_{\sharp 5}$

2 1 3 1 4
R

$B7^{\flat 9}_{\sharp 5}$
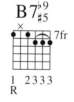
1   2 3 3 3
R

7fr

$B7^{\flat 9}_{\sharp 5}$
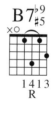
1 4 1 3
R

$B7^{\flat 9}_{\sharp 5}$
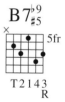
T 2 1 4 3
R

5fr

$B7^{\sharp 9}_{\sharp 11}$
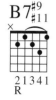
2 1 3 4 1
R

$B7^{\sharp 9}_{\sharp 11}$

2 1 3 4 1
R

6fr

$B7^{\sharp 9}_{\sharp 11}$
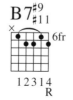
1 2 3 1 4
R

6fr

$B7^{\sharp 9}_{\sharp 11}$
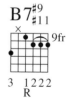
3   1 2 2 2
R

9fr

B

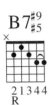

B7$^{\sharp 9}_{\sharp 5}$

2 1 3 4 4
R

B7$^{\sharp 9}_{\sharp 5}$

6fr

2 1 3 3 4
R

B7$^{\sharp 9}_{\sharp 5}$

6fr

1 2 2 4 3
R

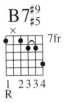

B7$^{\sharp 9}_{\sharp 5}$

7fr

1 2 3 3 4
R

Major Seventh (maj7, M7, ma7, △7)

Bmaj7

2 1 4
R

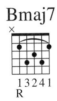

Bmaj7

1 3 2 4 1
R

Bmaj7

9fr

2 1 3 4
R

Bmaj7

4fr

1 1 1 4
R

Major Seventh Chords with Alterations

Bmaj7♭5

3 1 4 2
R

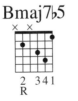

Bmaj7♭5

2 3 4 1
R

Bmaj7♭5

9fr

3 1 2 4
R

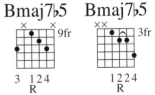

Bmaj7♭5

3fr

1 2 2 4
R

B

Bmaj7#5

2 1 3 4
R

Bmaj7#5

7fr

1   3 3 3
R

Bmaj7#5

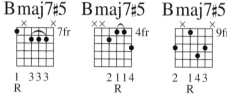

4fr

2 1 1 4
R

Bmaj7#5

9fr

2   1 4 3
R

Bmaj7$^{\sharp 9}_{\sharp 11}$

2 1 3 4 1
R

Bmaj7$^{\sharp 9}_{\sharp 11}$

6fr

2 1 4 3 1
R

Bmaj7$^{\sharp 9}_{\sharp 11}$

6fr

1 4 2 1 1
R

Bmaj7$^{\sharp 9}_{\sharp 11}$

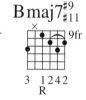

9fr

3   1 2 4 2
R

Minor Seventh (m7, min7, -7)

Bm7

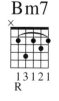

1 3 1 2 1
R

Bm7

7fr

1 3 1 1 1 1
R

Bm7

9fr

1 3 2 2
R

Bm7

2   3   4
R

B

Minor Seventh Chords with Alterations

Bm7♭5

Bm7♭5

Bm7♭5

Bm7♭5

Minor-Major Seventh [m(maj7), m/M7]

Bm(maj7)

Bm(maj7)

Bm(maj7)

Bm(maj7)

Diminished Seventh (°7)

B°7

B°7

B°7

B°7

B

Ninth Chords

Dominant Ninth (9)

B9

2 1 3 4
R

B9

6fr
2 1 3 1 4
R

B9

7fr
1 2   4
R

B9
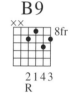
8fr
2 1 4 3
R

Dominant Ninth Chords with Alterations

B9♭5
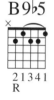
2 1 3 4 1
R

B9♭5
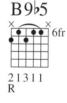
6fr
2 1 3 1 1
R

B9♭5

6fr
1 2 1 1 3
R

B9♭5
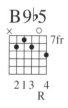
7fr
2 1 3   4
R

B9♯5

2 1 3 3 4
R

B9♯5

7fr
1   2 3 3 4
R

B9♯5

6fr
1 2 1 4 3
R

B9♯5

11fr
2 1 3 4 1
R

B

Major Ninth (maj9, M9, ma9, △9)

Bmaj9

× ×
2 1 4 3
R

Bmaj9

× 6fr
2 1 4 1 3
R

Bmaj9

× × 7fr
3 2 4 1
R

Bmaj9

× × ○ 8fr
1 2 4
R

Minor Ninth (m9, min9, -9)

Bm9

× ○
2 3 3 3
R

Bm9

7fr
1 3 1 1 1 4
R

Bm9

× × 5fr
3 1 4 2
R

Bm9

× × 7fr
2 1 4 3
R

Minor Ninth Chords with Alterations

Bm9♭5

× 5fr
1 3 2 2 4
R

Bm9♭5

7fr
1 2 1 1 4 3
R

Bm9♭5

× ○
2 3 4 1
R

Bm9♭5

× 7fr
T 2 1 4 3
R

B

Minor-Major Ninth [m(maj9), m/M9]

Bm(maj9)   Bm(maj9)   Bm(maj9)   Bm(maj9)

Eleventh Chords

Dominant Eleventh (11)

B11   B11   B11   B11

 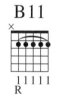

Major Eleventh (maj11, M11, ma11, △11)

Bmaj11   Bmaj11   Bmaj11   Bmaj11

B

Minor Eleventh (m11, min11, -11)

Bm11

2 3 4
R

Bm11

9fr
1 1 1 1 3 3
R

Bm11

5fr
3 1 4 2
R

Bm11

10fr
4 3 2 1

Thirteenth Chords

Dominant Thirteenth (13)

B 13

7fr
1 2 3 4 4
R

B 13

2 1 3 3 4
R

B 13

12fr
1 2 3
R

B 13

4fr
3 4 2 1 1
R

Dominant 13th Chords with Alterations

B 13#11

1 2 1 3 4
R

B 13#11

7fr
1 2 1 3 4
R

B 13#11

9fr
4 1 2 1 3
R

B 13#11
7fr
2 1 3 4 1
R

B

B13♭9

3 4 2 1 1
R

B13♭9

1 2 1 4

B13♭9

T 1 2 4 3
R

B13♭9

1 1 1

B13♯9

1 2 3 4

B13♯9

2 1 3 3 4
R

B13♯9

1 2 3 4

B13♯9

1 2 4

Major Thirteenth (maj13, M13, ma13, △13)

Bmaj13

1 2 3 4
R

Bmaj13

3 4 2 1 1
R

Bmaj13

1 2 3 4 4
R

Bmaj13

2 2 1 3 4 4
R

B

Major 13th Chords with Alterations

Bmaj13#11   Bmaj13#11   Bmaj13#11   Bmaj13#11

1 2 2 2 4
R

1 2 2 3 4
R

2   1 3 1 1
R

T 3 2 4 1
R

Minor Thirteenth (m13, min13, -13)

Bm13   Bm13   Bm13   Bm13

2   3 3 4 4
R

1 3 1 1 4 1
R

1 3 1 2 4
R

1   2 2 4
R

Minor 13th Chords with Alterations

Bm13♭5   Bm13♭5   Bm13♭5   Bm13♭5

1 2 1 1 4 1
R

1 2 1 3 4
R

1 1 2 1 3
R

2 4 1 3 1
R

B

Sixth Chords

Sixth Chords (6)

B6
× × 6fr
2 143
R

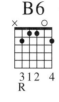
B6
× ○
312 4
R

B6
×
13333
R

B6
× ○ 6fr
413 2
R

Six-Nine Chords ($\frac{6}{9}$)

B$\frac{6}{9}$
×
21134
R

B$\frac{6}{9}$
× 6fr
11133
R

B$\frac{6}{9}$
× × 8fr
2134
R

B$\frac{6}{9}$
× ○ 6fr
312 4
R

Minor Sixth Chords (m6)

Bm6
× × 6fr
2 134
R

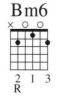
Bm6
× ○ ○
2 1 3
R

Bm6
× × 7fr
3141
R

Bm6
× × 9fr
1312
R

B

Minor Six-Nine Chords (m$_9^6$)

Bm$_9^6$

2 1 3 4
R

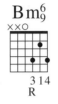
Bm$_9^6$

3 1 4
R

Bm$_9^6$
7fr

2 1 3 4
R

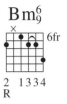
Bm$_9^6$
6fr

2 1 3 3 4
R

Power Chords ("5" Chords)

B 5

1 3 4
R

B 5
7fr

1 3 4
R

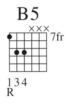
B 5

3 4   1
R

B 5
4fr

1 4 4
R

Suspended (sus) and add Chords

B sus2
9fr

1 3 4 1
R

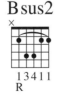
B sus2

1 3 4 1 1
R

B sus2
7fr

1 2 4
R

B sus2
6fr

4 1 2
R

B

B sus4

1 3 4
R

B sus4

9fr

1 3 4 4
R

B sus4

2fr

1 3 3 4
R

B sus4

7fr

1 1 3 4 1 1
R

B sus$_4^2$

1 3 4 2
R

B sus$_4^2$

4fr

4 1 3 2
R

B sus$_4^2$

9fr

1 1 4 1
R

B sus$_4^2$

7fr

2 3 1 4
R

B 7sus4

1 4 2
R

B 7sus4

9fr

1 3 2 4
R

B 7sus4

7fr

1 3 1 4 1 1
R

B 7sus4

4fr

2 3 1 4
R

B

B9sus4

× ○

1 4 1 2
R

B9sus4

6fr

2 2 1 3 4
R

B9sus4

× ×   9fr

1 1 2 1
R

B9sus4

× ×   5fr

3 2 1 4
R

B13sus4

7fr

1 1 1 3 4 1
R

B13sus4

×

1 1 1 1 4
R

B13sus4

× ○   ○ ○

4 1
R

B13sus4

×   9fr

4 1 1 1 1
R

Badd4

×   ○

1 2 3 4
R

Badd4

11fr

×

3 4 1 2 1
R

Badd4

○ ○   7fr

1 3 4 2
R

Badd4

× ×   ○   7fr

3 2 1
R

B

Badd9

3 2 1 4
R
11fr

Badd9

3 2 1 4
R
7fr

Badd9

2 3 1 4
R
8fr

Badd9

4 2 1 3
R
4fr

Bm(add9)

3 2 1 4
R
11fr

Bm(add9)

3 1 1 4
R
7fr

Bm(add9)

4 1 1 1
R
7fr

Bm(add9)

4 2 1 3
R
4fr

"No Third" Chords

B7(no 3rd)

1   2
R

B7(no 3rd)

2 3 4
R
7fr

B9(no 3rd)

3 2   4
R
6fr

B13(no 3rd)

1 1 4 2
R
9fr

B

Other Altered Chords

B(♭5)

1 2 3 4
R

B(♭5)
9fr
1 2 4 3
R

B(♭6)

2 1　　4
R

B(♭6)
7fr

1 4 3 2 1 1
R

Open Voice Triads

B
× ×　×
4fr

1 4　3
　R

B
× ×　×
9fr
1 3　4
R

Bm
× ×　×
4fr

1 3　4
　　R

Bm
× ×　×
7fr
3　1 4
R

B°
× ×
3fr

1 3　4
　R

B°
× ×　×
6fr
3　1 4
R

B+
× ×　×
5fr

1 4　3
　　R

B+
× ×　×
9fr

1 4　3
　R